FACING YOUR final JOB
REVIEW

THE JUDGMENT SEAT OF CHRIST, SALVATION, AND ETERNAL REWARDS

WOODROW KROLL

CROSSWAY BOOKS

WHEATON, ILLINOIS

Facing Your Final Job Review: The Judgment Seat of Christ, Salvation, and Eternal Rewards
Copyright © 2008 by Woodrow Kroll
Published by Crossway Books
        a publishing ministry of Good News Publishers
        1300 Crescent Street
        Wheaton, Illinois 60187

Interior design and typesetting by Lakeside Design Plus
Cover by The DesignWorks Group

First printing 2008
Printed in the United States of America

Scripture quotations are from *The Holy Bible, English Standard Version*™, copyright © 2001 by Crossway Bibles, a publishing ministry of Good News Publishers. Used by permission. All rights reserved.

Scripture references marked NKJV are from *The New King James Version*. Copyright © 1982, Thomas Nelson, Inc. Used by permission All emphases in Scripture quotations have been added by the author.

Library of Congress Cataloging-in-Publication Data
    Kroll, Woodrow Michael, 1944–
        Facing your final job review : the judgment seat of Christ, salvation, and eternal
    rewards / Woodrow Kroll.
        p. cm.
    Includes index.
    ISBN 978-1-58134-973-3 (tpb)
        1. Judgment Day. 2. Reward (Theology) 3. Salvation—Christianity. I. Title.

BT883.K76 2008
236'.9—dc22
                           2007030368

DP		16	15	14	13	12	11	10	09	08
		9	8	7	6	5	4	3	2	1

"As I've written and spoken about eternal rewards over the years, I've often wished this vital doctrine wasn't so ignored and misunderstood. Woodrow Kroll brings biblical clarity to this immensely important subject. I'm happy to recommend *Facing Your Final Job Review*."

—RANDY ALCORN, author of *The Law of Rewards* and *Heaven*

"The Judgment Seat of Christ is an event I studied very early in my Christian life—and have taught ever since. Why? Once the 'Job Review' is over, there's no going back and doing the job over! This is why the subject Wood has written about it so critical. How thankful I am for this timely and much needed book. May 2 Corinthians 5:9 become our ambition as a result of it."

—KAY ARTHUR, Bible teacher and Co-CEO of Precept Ministries International

"What a masterful book on such a misunderstood topic—the judgment seat of Christ. Kroll shows how 'starting every day at the judgment seat of Christ and working backwards' will infuse a new perspective and purpose for your life. This motivating book—filled with the biblical detail and insight we expect from Back to the Bible—will inspire you to be all, *yes* all, *that God created you to be!*"

—JUNE HUNT, Founder and CEO, Hope for the Heart

"Kroll makes a convincing case that the most important day of our lives is not in our past, but is yet to come. Are you ready? Perfect for anyone interested in what God's Word says about heaven, hell, and Bible prophecy. Readers will find clear direction and ample hope for their concerns in this life and the next."

—JOHN ANKERBERG, host of the *John Ankerberg Show*;
President and Founder, Ankerberg Theological Research Institute

"Woodrow Kroll packs a wealth of biblical insights into the often-neglected subject of future judgment and rewards. I highly recommend this book to all living in our instant-gratification society who wish to live 'today' in light of 'that day.' This is a sobering yet stimulating book that will encourage all followers of Christ to live lives pleasing to the Lord."

—JOHN H. MUNRO, Senior Pastor, Calvary Church, Charlotte, NC

"The best book I've ever read on the judgment seat of Christ. I say that because reading *Facing Your Final Job Review* made me think about that great day when I must stand before the Lord and give an account of my life. In a series of short, easily readable chapters, Kroll brings us face to face with the reality of rewards for the believer. What we do today counts for eternity. You'll never forget that once you've read this book."

—RAY PRITCHARD, President, Keep Believing Ministries;
author of *Credo*, *The Healing Power of Forgiveness*, and *Stealth Attack*

"Why haven't more people written on this subject, and why don't more Christians know about the practical implications of the *bēma* judgment seat of Christ? Now Woodrow Kroll has answered those questions by writing an extremely practical book to help every believer understand what he or she will face at the judgment seat of Christ.

If every believer read and understood that the final 'job review' will be the judgment seat of Christ, they would serve more faithfully and live more righteously. May God use this book to stimulate faithfulness in us all."

—ELMER L. TOWNS, Cofounder, Liberty University, Dean, School of Religion

"According to a recent religious survey poll, more books have been written during the past several decades on biblical prophecy than on any other subject. Much of the material in those books deal with the rapture of the church, the great tribulation, facts concerning the Antichrist, etc. Tragically, very little has been written in regard to what is undoubtedly the most important subject of all, namely, the judgment seat of Christ.

Dr. Kroll's book effectively bridges this gap, challenging all Christians to so order their lives today in light of that sobering 'Final Job Review' tomorrow. I cannot recommend this book too highly."

—H. L. WILMINGTON, Dean, Wilmington School of the Bible, Liberty University; author of *Wilmington's Guide to the Bible*

To my wife,
Linda.

Forever friend,
faithful fellow laborer,
and my greatest encouragement.

CONTENTS

ACKNOWLEDGMENTS

I WANT TO EXPRESS MY GRATITUDE to those who have assisted me in bringing this book to your attention.

First, there was that student who more than thirty-five years ago asked me a question about what Jesus would be looking for at the judgment seat and launched me on a lifelong quest to better understand this important event.

Then there was the always valuable editorial assistance of my friends at Back to the Bible International, Tami Weissert and Allen Bean, and the checking of the manuscript by my administrative assistant Cathy Strate.

Of course, no book gets into your hands without a publisher. My thanks to Lane Dennis, president and publisher of Crossway Books, to Allan Fisher, senior vice president for book publishing, and to Tara Davis, editor.

Primarily I want to acknowledge the Lord Jesus, "who loved me and gave himself for me," without whom there would be no reason for the judgment seat of Christ.

Introduction

THE MOST IMPORTANT DAY IN YOUR FUTURE

*"Do you not think that it would make a difference to you
if you really believed the thrilling consciousness that every
act of the present was registered, and would tell, on the far
side beyond?"—Alexander Maclaren*

WHILE BEING INTERVIEWED on radio once I was asked, "What's the most important day in your life?" I thought for a minute before I answered. October 21 is my birthday, so that was a biggie. My wife, Linda, and I were married June 26, 1965; surely that day impacted everything. And, obviously, there was that cold, snowy night when I was five years old and walked down the aisle in a little country church to trust Christ as my Savior. That day changed my life forever.

But before I could get my answer out, the interviewer clarified, "I mean, what's the most important day *yet* in your life? What's the most important day in your future?" Oooh. That will take some more thought.

Maybe the day I die. Certainly that day will bring big changes to me. Or what about the day the Lord returns? That's an important day in the future. Have you done any thinking about this question yourself? What's the most important day you have yet to face? If you could single out one day in the eternity that awaits you, which day would be the most important?

I discovered the answer in the Bible. The most important day in my future, the day that will have the greatest impact on eternity for me, is the day I stand before the judgment seat of Christ. And, if you're a follower of Christ like me, that's the most important day in your future, too.

So, how much do you know about that day? What is the judgment seat of Christ? What will happen there, and what impact will it have on the never-ending years of eternity? Good questions. Do you know the answers?

If you're at all a little fuzzy about the where, when, why, and so on of the judgment seat of Christ, you've picked up the right book. We're going to answer all those questions, and we're going to answer them from the Bible.

For example, did you know that the Bible mentions two future judgments? One of them is the judgment seat of Christ, which we're going to talk about. The other is the great white throne judgment mentioned in Revelation 20:11–15. One judgment will be glorious; the other will be horrific. One will open eons of eternity in heaven; the other will open eons of eternity in hell. One brings reward; the other brings punishment. At the judgment seat of Christ, the RSVP is only for people of faith, those who have trusted Jesus Christ as their Savior. At the great white throne judgment, only unbelievers, those who have rejected Jesus, will be ordered to appear.

The Judgment Seat of Christ

This book is about the judgment seat of Christ, salvation, and eternal rewards. Those are not three randomly-chosen subjects. They are as interrelated as Athos, Porthos, and Aramis (the Three Musketeers) or José Carreras, Plácido Domingo, and Luciano Pavarotti (the three tenors).

The judgment seat of Christ is the place where every Christ-follower will one day stand. Our salvation is our ticket. We will be there because of what Christ Jesus did when he saved us. No one who has failed to come to grips with his sin will be invited. No one who has refused to exercise faith alone in Christ alone will be present. In fact, all who have rejected Christ as Savior have their own judgment—at the great white throne. The judgment seat of Christ is the believer's judgment. Only those who have been born again will stand there. This is a day for people of faith.

Eternal Rewards

The reason Christ-followers stand before this judgment seat is to have our lives evaluated. It is to have the service we've done for the Lord Jesus appraised and, for what's deemed acceptable, compensated. This is where eternal rewards are awarded for faithful service. This is where the Master says, "Well done." This is where the determination is made of what we will enjoy for all eternity. Now if that's not the most important day in your future, I don't know what is.

But if what we enjoy for all eternity is judged acceptable at the judgment seat of Christ, don't you think we ought to know now what the Judge is looking for, rather than to wait until then to find out? Makes sense, doesn't it?

At the judgment seat of Christ our eternal rewards are determined and awarded based on the criteria established by God himself. So what is he looking for? What criteria will Jesus use when he judges your life and your service? Don't you think it's a little risky not to be sure? We're talking about *eternal* rewards here. I want to know now what he's looking for then so if I need to I can make some adjustments in my life.

But a huge question remains: If our eternal rewards are determined at the judgment seat of Christ, isn't the most important issue you face right now making sure you stand before this judgment seat and not the great white throne judgment? That makes sense, too.

Salvation

Eternal rewards are determined at the judgment seat of Christ. But the judgment seat is dependent on our salvation. So what do we have to do to be saved?

That's a question people have been asking for a long time. When the apostle Paul was thrown into jail in the city of Philippi in northern Greece, and an earthquake jolted open all the prison doors, the jailer was about to commit suicide thinking all his prisoners had escaped. When Paul assured him they were still there, the jailed asked the most important question anyone can ask: "What must I do to be saved?" (Acts 16:30). That's the question we're asking here.

Once a young rich man who was a religious leader in Israel came to Jesus and asked a similar question: "Good Teacher, what must I do to inherit eternal life?" (Luke 18:18). Jesus directed the man's thinking to whether he had kept all the commandments. The man had done his best, but he knew something was still lacking. Salvation never comes by keeping commandments, doing good things, or hoping your good works outweigh your bad.

Do you see what's wrong with both the Philippian jailer's and the young religious leader's questions? They assume there is something you must *do* in order to be saved from sin. Fact is, there is nothing you can do. Paul describes us as being "dead in the trespasses and sins" of our life (Eph. 2:1). Not sick, dead. What can a person who is spiritually dead do to earn salvation? Nothing. Dead means dead. You can't even lift a little finger to save yourself. If you're to be saved from sin, salvation must come from outside of you.

That's why the gospel is such good news. The gospel is the story of Jesus' death, burial, and resurrection. What you can't do, Jesus already did for you. When Paul responded to the jailer's query, "What must I do to be saved?" the apostle said, "Believe in the Lord Jesus, and you will be saved..." (Acts 16:31). It's not what you do that brings salvation; it's what Jesus has already done for you.

When Jesus died on the cross, he didn't belong there. He hadn't sinned. He wasn't guilty of anything. Pilate knew that (John 19:4, 6); the centurion knew that (Luke 23:47); God knew that. "For our sake he [God the Father] made him [God the Son] to be sin who knew no sin, so that in him we might become the righteousness of God" (2 Cor. 5:21). Jesus was dying in your place, for your sin. He paid a debt he didn't owe because you owed a debt you couldn't pay.

What's in Your Future?

Before you begin reading about the judgment seat of Christ you have to ask yourself, is this the judgment in my future? If only those who have trusted Christ as Savior appear before the judgment seat of Christ for reward, and all others must appear before the great white throne for punishment, how do I know I am headed for the right judgment?

The answer is faith. "Believe in the Lord Jesus, and you will be saved." The only requirement God makes for you to enjoy eternity in heaven is to have faith that what Jesus did for you at Calvary is all that God required to pay the penalty for your sins. It's not a matter of getting your life in order. It's not undoing all your bad karma. It's simple faith, the kind of faith a little child would have.

If you're not certain you're saved, here's what you should do, right now, before you read any further.

1. Acknowledge that you have sinned against a holy God and that you know there are bad consequences to your bad actions (Rom. 3:23). Genuinely feel the pain of your sin and be willing to turn from it (repent) and give God free access to your life (Acts 3:19).

2. Believe in your heart and mind that Jesus is the Son of God, that he died on the cross for you (John 3:1–18) in your place, and was raised back to life blazing a trail for you to follow when you die. There is no one else you can turn to (John 14:6). "There is salvation in no one else, for there is no other name under heaven given among men by which we must be saved" (Acts 4:12).

3. Confess that you are trusting Jesus as your personal Savior. Since Jesus is alive, you can talk to him. This is called prayer. So talk to him right now, in your own words, and accept his invitation to know him. Invite him not just to save you from hell but to take control of your life as the One who has saved you (Rom. 6:23; 10:9–10).

There. It's really as simple as A-B-C. If you followed the steps above and sincerely meant it, you have encountered Jesus in a saving way. You have been born again, born from above. "For by grace you have been saved through faith. And this is not your own doing; it is the gift of God, not a result of works, so that no one may boast" (Eph. 2:8–9). You have become a follower of Christ. Now you're ready for the next verse, Ephesians 2:10: "For we are his workmanship, created in Christ Jesus for good works, which God prepared beforehand, that we should walk in them."

What you do can never save you. But once you are saved, what you do plays a huge role in what happens when you stand before the judgment seat of Christ. God saved you for a purpose—to glorify him through your life. It's that life of service that will be evaluated at the judgment seat of Christ and, when found acceptable, will bring you eternal rewards.

So, are you ready? Salvation first. Then the judgment seat. Then eternal rewards. Are you ready to stand before the judgment seat of Christ? What do you have to show for your life here on earth? Jesus said, "Do not lay up for yourselves treasures on earth, where moth and rust destroy and where thieves break in and steal, but lay up for yourselves treasures in heaven, where neither moth nor rust destroys and where thieves do not break in and steal. For where your treasure is, there your heart will be also" (Matt. 6:19–21).

It's true that you can't take it with you, but you can send it on ahead. Are you satisfied that you've done all you should have done before it's too late?

Prologue

It's Too Late Now

"We'll have all eternity to celebrate our victories, but only one short hour before sunset to win them."—Robert Moffat

WHO WAS REALLY READY? *None of us! We had been waiting for this day, sung about it, read about it, longingly anticipated it; but when it finally came, we were caught completely off guard.*

There was so much more to do. We had so many good intentions, so many good plans. There were study groups to meet, events to be planned, outreach programs to be organized. Our church had just initiated a ten-year strategic plan. We had so much potential for growth. Now, all those plans, those preparations and programs, all that potential, is meaningless.

I know this should be the happiest day of my life, but I'm so apprehensive. Oh sure, the instant it happened, my mind was overwhelmed with wonder. To think that after years of anticipation and anxious waiting, I have actually experienced the Lord's return! I am with him! He really did come back, as he said he would.

A split second ago I heard the deafening blast of the trumpet. The sweetest voice ever heard called me to come up to him. Jesus Christ has returned and now time has yielded to eternity. It all happened before you could bat an eyelash, and I was astonished.

Yet, with so much to think about, my mind still slips back to the colossal amount of things I had planned to do. Trying to tell myself not to worry about them, or even think about them, just doesn't work. What I could have done for the Lord and didn't do will now never get done. I just can't put this out of my mind.

I keep asking myself, "Why didn't I do more when I had the chance? What was the matter with me?" *I knew better. Why did I spend so much time on foolish things? How could I have allowed my service to the Lord to be so minimal? But all this questioning is useless.* "Forgive me. Please forgive me, Lord Jesus, for letting other things take up so much of my time. Forgive me for not getting around to all the things I knew I should be doing. Forgive me, for it's too late now!"

The world has not yet witnessed this agonizing drama, but it's as certain as sunrise that one day it will. That day cannot be far off. Jesus Christ is coming back for his church, and most of us aren't ready. Soon, in a split second, in the twinkling of an eye, life as we know it is going to change forever, and we will be caught up into the air to meet him. It will all happen so fast. It will all be so final.

But does this knowledge make any difference? Does the possibility of facing a scenario like this tomorrow change anything you do in the next twenty-four hours? For most of us it likely won't. We believe in the Lord's return, but we live each day as if it weren't really going to happen.

Maybe if we had a keener appreciation for how quick and final that day will be we would drastically change our plans for tomorrow. If we caught a glimpse of that day and what follows it, maybe—just maybe—we would have a greater sense of urgency in how we live for Jesus now.

Facing Your Final Job Review explores the reality of the judgment seat of Christ. This largely neglected teaching is the real "sleeper" in our Christian thinking. While playing a major role in our future, it has been pushed to the back burner of our minds. That's the way Satan wants it.

In this book, we're going to bring the subject to the front burner and turn up the heat. We want to see how important our court date at the judgment seat is and how knowing this day is "out there" should shape our lives today. We need to work diligently, faithfully, and fruitfully for Jesus now because, after all, when it's too late, it's too late!

PART ONE

Salvation and Rewards

Most of us are familiar with job reviews. Regardless of your occupation or career, you've probably survived a job review or two. Generally, at least once a year your supervisor calls you into his office and evaluates your work performance. There you sit, fidgeting, with sweaty palms, wondering whether your boss will be pleased and reward you or, with the skill of a surgeon, he will slice and dice you, and there will be no pay raise, no bonus, no promotion.

But there's one job review that's more significant than any you've faced in your career. It's the job review that takes place as you stand before the judgment seat of Christ, and the Lord Jesus reviews your performance as a Christian. Because this event is so crucial to eternity, we need to get a handle on what the judgment seat is and what the Judge will be looking for when reviewing our job performance.

Of all the questions people ask about the judgment seat of Christ, eternal rewards, and the future, perhaps the ones that reveal the most confusion are related to the difference between salvation and rewards. It's easy to see how this could be so confusing. Those who understand the Bible rightly never use the word "work" in the context of salvation. Yet when we talk about facing our final job review, we often speak of working for rewards. If working plays no role in our salvation, why does it play a role in our eternal rewards? That's a good question and one we will address in this first section of *Facing Your Final Job Review*.

1

WHAT IS GOD'S SALVATION?

"There is no inconsistency in saying that God rewards good works, provided we understand that, nevertheless, men obtain eternal life gratuitously."—John Calvin

FOR THOSE OF US who have come to believe that salvation is by grace alone, through faith alone, in Christ alone, it is sometimes difficult to square salvation with the concept of rewards. They just don't seem compatible. So, to demonstrate that salvation is not itself a reward, consider these facts. Salvation is provided for all sinners and is the same for all sinners. Salvation is God's gracious gift to us, and it is a present possession. Salvation is not earned, and it is not universal. It is God's unique gift to us.

Since we're answering questions about eternal rewards in this book, it will be good for us first to spend some time thinking about how eternal rewards differ from our eternal salvation. If we're confused here, we'll not see rewards in the same way the Bible does.

Salvation Is Provided for Sinners

One of the fundamental precepts in the history of God's salvation for humans is that everyone—no matter who he or she is—needs salvation. The Bible depicts humans as rebellious creatures who chose to disobey their Creator. Given the opportunity to live in a perfect, pollution-free environment in harmony with God and nature, Adam and Eve instead listened to the faulty advice of Satan and rebelled against God. Thus the fellowship that was such an important part of their Eden relationship with God was lost. Humans became alienated from God, separated from fellowship with their Creator. People no longer enjoyed God or his company.

But God's plan has always been to redeem men and women from their sin. The God who created us and owned us would buy us back from the bondage of sin we had fallen into. He would do this through the payment of a ransom, the blood of his own Son. God would restore us to the divine fellowship that we lost, and he would renew our mind so that we could understand the things of God and live at peace with him. Thus, salvation is provided to sinners:

- **John 1:12:** "But to all who did receive him, who believed in his name, he gave the right to become children of God."
- **Luke 19:10:** "For the Son of Man came to seek and to save the lost."
- **Romans 5:8–9:** "But God shows his love for us in that while we were still sinners, Christ died for us. Since, therefore, we have now been justified by his blood, much more shall we be saved by him from the wrath of God."
- **Romans 6:23:** "For the wages of sin is death, but the free gift of God is eternal life in Christ Jesus our Lord."
- **Galatians 3:22:** "But the Scripture imprisoned everything under sin, so that the promise by faith in Jesus Christ might be given to those who believe."
- **1 Timothy 1:15:** "The saying is trustworthy and deserving of full acceptance, that Christ Jesus came into the world to save sinners, of whom I am the foremost."

Salvation Is the Same for All Sinners

A major tool in law enforcement has become the science of DNA testing; the genetic code of our DNA reveals that we are distinct individuals. This is true for all of God's creation. No two snowflakes, trees, or blades of grass are exactly the same.

When people are miraculously born again by the Spirit of God, the circumstances from which they are saved aren't identical to those of any other person. Some have not committed felonies or serious crimes. Others have. Some haven't stolen from their parents or robbed a convenience store. Others have. Some haven't slept with a different person each night. Others have. Some have never set foot inside a church. Many have.

The backgrounds from which God calls and saves his people are not at all identical. Many times they're not even similar. If salvation depended on the effort of the individual, some would have to strive much harder to gain it. Their salvation would be a much greater achievement. But this has never been the case. Salvation does not depend on us. Salvation is the gracious act of God whereby he lifts us out of the horrible pit of sin, cleanses our life, and establishes us on the solid rock—Christ Jesus (Ps. 40:1–3).

Salvation is deep enough and full enough to cover completely the most terrible sinner as well as the sinner who has committed crimes judged less heinous by our society. God's salvation is the same to every man, woman, and child who receives it, because God is the same to all who receive him.

- **Malachi 3:6**: "For I the LORD do not change; therefore you, O children of Jacob, are not consumed."
- **Acts 13:37–39**: "But he whom God raised up did not see corruption. Let it be known to you therefore, brothers, that through this man forgiveness of sins is proclaimed to you, and by him everyone who believes is freed from everything from which you could not be freed by the law of Moses."
- **2 Corinthians 5:17**: "Therefore, if anyone is in Christ, he is a new creation. The old has passed away; behold, the new has come."

- **Hebrews 13:8**: "Jesus Christ is the same yesterday and today and forever."
- **James 1:17**: "Every good gift and every perfect gift is from above, coming down from the Father of lights with whom there is no variation or shadow due to change."

Salvation Is God's Gracious Gift

Basic to a biblical understanding of salvation is the fact that salvation is a free gift from God. People are saved by the grace of God, by trusting that Jesus' death paid the price for all the things they've done wrong. Salvation is gracious in that it is provided for us apart from any personal merit. No honest person can advance one good reason why he or she should be the objects of God's love and salvation. I know I can't, and I'm pretty sure you can't either. This can be chalked up only to God's grace. God, who is all-worthy, saves mankind, who is unworthy. Such is the grace of our God.

Paul describes salvation to his friends in Rome, acknowledging that "all have sinned and fall short of the glory of God" (Rom. 3:23), but that we "are justified by his grace as a gift, through the redemption that is in Christ Jesus" (v. 24). Don't miss the "power words" in that short phrase. We are justified (made right before God) by his grace (not by something we do), as a gift (the original word means without strings attached or no prior conditions having been met) through the redemption (ransom paid) that comes to us in Christ Jesus. Not much room for us to take any credit there.

Salvation is a gift; not only is it unmerited by our self-worth, it is not earned by our labors. You can't earn a gift. But you can thankfully receive it. The fact that salvation cannot be earned is clearly the teaching of the following verses:

- **Romans 6:23**: "For the wages of sin is death, but the free gift of God is eternal life in Christ Jesus our Lord."
- **Ephesians 2:8–9**: "For by grace you have been saved through faith. And this is not your own doing; it is the gift of God, not a result of works, so that no one may boast."

- **2 Timothy 1:9**: "Who saved us and called us to a holy calling, not because of our works but because of his own purpose and grace, which he gave us in Christ Jesus before the ages began."

Salvation Is a Present Possession

The Bible speaks of salvation as past, present, and future. We have been saved from the penalty of sin at the time of our new birth (Eph. 2:5, 8); we are presently being saved from the power of sin in our lives (Rom. 6:14); and one day we will be saved from the very presence of sin (Rom. 8:23). It is important to realize that salvation is not only a future possession. It is real in the life of those who follow Christ at this present moment. You and I don't look forward to the day when our sins will be forgiven: they have already been forgiven.

If salvation were not a present possession, we could do no valid service for God now that would earn a reward later. Salvation must precede service. It is presently and permanently ours by God's grace. Notice in the following verses how salvation is always spoken of in the present tense:

- **John 3:36**: "Whoever believes in the Son has eternal life; whoever does not obey the Son shall not see life, but the wrath of God remains on him."
- **John 5:24**: "Truly, truly, I say to you, whoever hears my word and believes him who sent me has eternal life. He does not come into judgment, but has passed from death to life."
- **John 6:47–48**: "Truly, truly, I say to you, whoever believes has eternal life. I am the bread of life."
- **1 John 5:11–12**: "And this is the testimony, that God gave us eternal life, and this life is in his Son. Whoever has the Son has life; whoever does not have the Son of God does not have life."

Salvation is God's pure act of grace, motivated by his perfect love, whereby he paid the penalty for your sin through Jesus' death on the cross and invites you to receive the benefit of Christ's death freely when you come to grips with your sin and express faith in Christ.

It just doesn't get any better than that!

2

HOW ARE REWARDS DIFFERENT FROM SALVATION?

"Blood washed believers will be spotless in God's sight, but not all will have the same service record. God is after obedience. Salvation gets us to heaven, but works determine what we do after we get there."—C. S. Lovett

THINK OF THINGS that stand in opposition to each other. Ford drivers don't buy Chevys. Pepsi drinkers don't drink Coke. Mac users never consider buying a PC. You're either a Yankees' fan or a Mets' fan, but not a fan of both. Democrats see Republicans as elitist, right-wing conspirators. Republicans see Democrats as spendthrift socialists. Let's face it: this world has a lot of contrasts that we deal with every day.

The same thing is true in your spiritual life. Standing in contrast to the believer's salvation are the believer's rewards. By carefully examining the character of our rewards and contrasting that with the character of our salvation, we can easily see the sharp distinction.

Rewards Are Awarded to Saints

Salvation is provided for sinners. In contrast, eternal rewards are awarded to saints. So what is a saint? In some religious traditions the church honors the life of certain people by declaring, after they are dead, that they have attained such a high degree of blessedness they deserve to be called saints. This is called beatification, and was applied to many of the early church fathers such as Ambrose, Augustine, and Bernard of Clairvaux. But the New Testament word "saint" always refers to a believer who has been set apart to serve God. So, if you've trusted Jesus Christ as your personal Savior—if you're a follower of Christ—you are a saint.

Unlike salvation, which is applied to the lives of sinners, rewards are given to saints at the judgment seat of Christ. These rewards are reserved for believer-saints and for them alone. Just as a person cannot receive a paycheck until he or she is legally and gainfully employed, so also a person cannot receive God's rewards until he or she becomes God's servant.

- **Luke 6:22–23**: "Blessed are you when people hate you and when they exclude you and revile you and spurn your name as evil, on account of the Son of Man! Rejoice in that day, and leap for joy . . . for so their fathers did to the prophets."
- **1 Corinthians 9:24**: "Do you not know that in a race all the runners run, but only one receives the prize? So run that you may obtain it."
- **Ephesians 2:8–10**: "For by grace you have been saved through faith. And this is not your own doing; it is the gift of God, not a result of works, so that no one may boast. For we are his workmanship, created in Christ Jesus for good works, which God prepared beforehand, that we should walk in them."

Rewards Are Proportionate to Service

Remember, salvation is the same for everyone. The Bible speaks of just two classes of people. These are not the black or white, rich or poor, moral or immoral. These classes are saved and lost—those who have trusted God's Son as their Savior and those who have not. The apostle John said it this way: "Whoever has the Son has life; whoever does not have the Son of God does not have life" (1 John 5:12). Either you are completely, wonderfully saved, or you are completely, hopelessly lost.

Unlike salvation, however, there are varying degrees of rewards. Some will receive great rewards, others will not. Our rewards are proportionate to our acceptable service.

You may remember the Enron scandal. While the company's leaders were dumping their Enron stock, they assured their employees that the company was sound. When Enron filed for Chapter 11 bankruptcy, pension plans and lenders were left with at least $5 billion at risk. More than four thousand Enron employees lost their jobs and their 401(k) savings.

Enron's top three executives all went to jail, but they didn't all receive the same length of sentences. Jeffrey Skilling, a former Enron CEO, was convicted of federal felony charges and is serving a twenty-four-year, four-month prison sentence. Kenneth Lay, CEO and chairman of Enron at the time of its collapse, was found guilty on ten counts of conspiracy and fraud and could have faced twenty to thirty years in prison. However, Lay died of a heart attack before he was sentenced. Andrew Fastow, Enron's chief financial officer, was largely behind the complex web of limited partnerships that Enron controlled and used to conceal the massive losses. He is serving a prison sentence of sixty years, followed by two years of probation. The difference in the prison sentences reflects the judge's understanding of the degree of guilt each man bore.

There have always been degrees of punishment in just societies. This concept is seen in one of the great masterpieces of literature, Dante Alighieri's *La Divina Commedia* (*The Divine Comedy*).[1] Dante wrote his work in three parts, or canticles. (A canticle is a hymn from the Bible.) In his first part, the *Inferno*, Dante depicts hell as having deepening circles of condemnation and punishment. The more horrific your sin, the more torturous your punishment for eternity.

The concept of a more sever punishment for a more sever sin and greater reward for greater service is a biblical concept. Frequently Jesus Christ spoke of rewards in proportion to labor, counseling his disciples to labor for a "great" reward. John speaks of a "full" reward. If such adjectives as "full" and "great" can be used to describe our rewards, then not all rewards are alike, as these verses indicate:

- **Matthew 16:27**: "For the Son of man is going to come with his angels in the glory of his Father, and then he will repay each person according to what he has done."
- **Luke 12:47–48**: "And that servant who knew his master's will but did not get ready or act according to his will, will receive a severe beating. But the one who did not know, and did what deserved a beating, will receive a light beating. Everyone to whom much was given, of him much will be required, and from him to whom they entrusted much, they will demand the more."
- **1 Corinthians 3:8**: "He who plants and he who waters are one, and each will receive his wages according to his labor."
- **2 Corinthians 5:10**: "For we must all appear before the judgment seat of Christ, so that each one may receive what is due for what he has done in the body, whether good or evil."
- **1 Timothy 5:18**: "For the Scripture says, 'You shall not muzzle an ox when it treads out the grain,' and 'The laborer deserves his wages.'"

Rewards Are a Gracious Wage

Remember from our last chapter that salvation is a gracious gift. The Bible teaches we are saved by grace, through faith, plus nothing! This means that we are saved by grace apart from works. Yet, after we have been born again to a new life in Christ, we are to engage in the good works that Jesus himself has prepared for us in advance (Eph. 2:8–10).

Rewards are given to us for faithful service rendered after salvation. The reward is a wage paid in respect to the service performed. If no service is performed, or if it is unacceptable service, no wage is paid.

After Hurricane Katrina ripped through the Gulf Coast of the United States, those homes that weren't entirely destroyed were often severely damaged. Suppose one of them were your house. If you needed a roof repaired, and some guy showed up on your street with a pickup saying he was a professional roofer and would fix your roof, would you pay him upfront before he did any work? Of course not. Payment comes after work is done, not before. If the work he did was unacceptable, or only partially complete, would you pay him in full? No, you wouldn't. Wages are the promise of work completed satisfactorily.

Can you earn a reward for your service to God? Yes, but it's only by God's infinite grace that you can perform any acceptable service at all. Your reward, then, is a gracious wage paid for being a willing and useful servant. Unlike salvation, of which we are but recipients, we are active participants in earning our reward.

- **1 Corinthians 9:24–25**: "Do you not know that in a race all the runners run but only one receives the prize? So run that you may obtain it. Every athlete exercises self-control in all things. They do it to receive a perishable wreath, but we an imperishable."
- **2 Timothy 4:6–8**: "For I am already being poured out as a drink offering, and the time of my departure has come. I have fought the good fight, I have finished the race, I have kept the faith. Henceforth there is laid up for me the crown of righteousness, which the Lord, the righteous judge, will award to me on that Day, and not only to me but also to all who have loved his appearing."
- **Revelation 22:12**: "Behold, I am coming soon, bringing my recompense with me, to repay everyone for what he has done."

Rewards Are a Future Possession

In contrast to salvation, which the Bible indicates is enjoyed now, eternal rewards are reserved for the future. Eternal rewards are awarded only as a result of your service being judged acceptable. That won't happen until the judgment seat of Christ, and since that's still a future event, your eternal rewards are future rewards.

This is not to say that we don't presently enjoy many blessings in serving Jesus. We do. There's great pleasure in pleasing the One who loved us and gave himself for us. But the blessings we now enjoy are only temporal blessings—things like good health, amiable friends, passion for our work, or fulfillment in doing a good job. They are not eternal rewards. There's a big difference. It is satisfying to know that we are doing the will of the Lord. This knowledge brings great comfort and blessing. But it is not a reward like having the Lord himself say, "Well done, good and faithful servant."

Notice how Paul speaks of rewards as a future attainment:

- **1 Corinthians 3:14**: "If the work that anyone has built on the foundation survives, he will receive a reward."
- **2 Timothy 4:7–8**: "I have fought the good fight, I have finished the race, I have kept the faith. Henceforth there is laid up for me the crown of righteousness, which the Lord, the righteous judge, will award to me on that Day, and not only to me but also to all who have loved his appearing."

Our Lord also speaks of rewards as a future attainment:

- **Matthew 16:27**: "For the Son of Man is going to come with his angels in the glory of his Father, and then he will repay each person according to what he has done."
- **Luke 14:14**: "And you will be blessed, because they cannot repay you. For you will be repaid at the resurrection of the just."

So, do you see that salvation and rewards are very different things?

- Salvation is provided for the sinner; rewards are awarded to the saint.
- Salvation is identical for all who by faith receive it; rewards are different for each person because they are proportionate to our life of service.

- Salvation is a gracious gift, given by God to the lost; rewards are a gracious wage paid by God to those who are saved.
- Salvation is now, to be enjoyed forever; rewards are not received until the race is won and we are in the presence of our great Reward Giver, God himself.
- Salvation is by faith, but the evaluation of our service is by works.

As we progress through this book together, the distinction between salvation and rewards will become even clearer. For now, make sure in your own life that the judgment seat of Christ is on your future agenda. It is if you've placed your faith in Jesus Christ as your Savior. That's where you must begin your journey to eternity.

3

SHOULD I BE CONCERNED ABOUT ETERNAL REWARDS?

"The Christian doctrine of reward is too often lost sight of or kept in abeyance, as if it were not perfectly consistent with the freest bestowment of heavenly glory."—John Eadie

IN THE LAST CHAPTER I mentioned the Enron scandal that rocked the financial world in the early years of the twenty-first century. Although the charges against the Enron executives were conspiracy, fraud, and making false statements, the underlying problem was just plain old greed.

First listed by Pope Gregory the Great (AD 540–604) and later in Dante's epic poem, *The Divine Comedy,* the so-called "seven deadly sins" are like the FBI's Most Wanted List of transgressions. Although all of these deadly sins are present in our world today, none of them is more so than greed.[1]

In the wake of the Enron debacle, Alan Greenspan, then chairman of the Federal Reserve Board, told a senate banking committee in Washington that "infectious greed" had gripped the business community and that "too many corporate executives sought ways to harvest some of those stock market gains." Greenspan added, "It is not that humans have become any more greedy than in generations past. It is that the avenues to express greed have grown so enormously."[2]

With greed so prevalent in the world today, it's legitimate for Christ-followers to be concerned about wanting to earn eternal rewards. Won't just making it to heaven be reward enough? Shouldn't that satisfy us? Why should we care about tangible rewards? After all, it seems so greedy to think about receiving payment for serving the Savior.

If you're part of the paid workforce in this country, you may enjoy your job and the team you work with and you may even get a sense of accomplishment from what you do, but without your paycheck, you'd be looking elsewhere for work. We all look forward to getting paid for two reasons: (1) we feel we've worked for it, and we've got it coming to us; and (2) we can't pay our bills without some form of income.

But should we view our eternal rewards the same way? There are those who argue, "I don't think we ought to talk about our rewards. Salvation is by grace, and it sounds so mercenary to be talking about rewards." That sounds spiritual, but it isn't biblical. There is nothing mercenary about eternal rewards. It's thoroughly scriptural, and we have every right to talk about our rewards and every reason to anticipate them. Here's why.

Rewards Are a Frequent Theme in Scripture

You may be surprised how often the Bible addresses rewards. So if the Bible is interested in the subject of rewards, don't you think we should be, too? Think about the Old Testament examples below. These verses are not exhaustive but are representative examples of how God rewards the faithfulness of his servants:

- **Genesis 15:1**: "After these things the word of the LORD came to Abram in a vision: 'Fear not, Abram, I am your shield; your reward shall be very great.'"
- **Ruth 2:12:** "The LORD repay you for what you have done, and a full reward be given you by the LORD, the God of Israel, under whose wings you have come to take refuge!"

- **1 Samuel 24:19:** "For if a man finds his enemy, will he let him go away safe? So may the LORD reward you with good for what you have done to me this day."
- **Psalm 19:9–11:** "The rules of the LORD are true, and righteous altogether. More to be desired are they than gold, even much fine gold; sweeter also than honey and drippings of the honeycomb. Moreover, by them is your servant warned; in keeping them there is great reward."
- **Psalm 58:11:** "Surely there is a reward for the righteous; surely there is a God who judges on earth."
- **Isaiah 62:11:** "Behold, the LORD has proclaimed to the end of the earth: Say to the daughter of Zion, 'Behold, your salvation comes; behold, his reward is with him, and his recompense before him.'"

The New Testament is even more enthusiastic about rewards. Consider these verses:

- **Matthew 5:12:** "Rejoice and be glad, for your reward is great in heaven, for so they persecuted the prophets who were before you."
- **Matthew 6:3–4:** "But when you give to the needy, do not let your left hand know what your right hand is doing, so that your giving may be in secret. And your Father who sees in secret will reward you."
- **Matthew 10:41:** "The one who receives a prophet because he is a prophet will receive a prophet's reward, and the one who receives a righteous person because he is a righteous person will receive a righteous person's reward."
- **Matthew 16:27:** "For the Son of Man is going to come with his angels in the glory of his Father, and then he will repay each person according to what he has done."
- **Mark 9:41:** "For truly, I say to you, whoever gives you a cup of water to drink because you belong to Christ will by no means lose his reward."

- **Luke 23:40–41:** "Do you not fear God, since you are under the same sentence of condemnation? And we indeed justly, for we are receiving the due reward of our deeds; but this man had done nothing wrong."
- **Colossians 3:23–24:** "Whatever you do, work heartily, as for the Lord and not for men, knowing that from the Lord you will receive the inheritance as your reward. You are serving the Lord Christ."
- **1 Timothy 5:18:** "For the Scripture says, 'You shall not muzzle an ox when it treads out the grain,' and, 'The laborer deserves his wages.'"
- **2 John 8:** "Watch yourselves, so that you may not lose what we have worked for, but may win a full reward."

The Bible doesn't avoid the subject of rewards, and neither should we. Paul told us we are to think about "whatever is true, whatever is honorable, whatever is just, whatever is pure, whatever is lovely, whatever is commendable" (Phil. 4:8), and God-given rewards surely fall into these categories.

Rewards Confirm Our Salvation

When Christ died for us on Calvary's cross, he cried out, "It is finished" (John 19:30), because all that needed to be done to pay the penalty for our sin us was complete. He paid in full our debt. Three days later, his resurrection proved that God had accepted his Son's sacrifice on our behalf. Redemption was accomplished.

If you've ever listened to me on radio you've probably heard me say, "You should never quote Ephesians 2:8–9." And then, after a long, agonizing pause I continue, "without quoting verse 10." Ephesians 2:10 gives the purpose for our salvation recorded in verses 8 and 9. Why is the believer in Christ saved from sin? To live a life filled with meaningful and enjoyable service to the one who saved us. The reason we have been given new life in Christ is to apply all that we have and all that we are toward a useful life for our Savior. This is what brings glory to God.

As author Randy Alcorn notes,

Somewhere we've gotten the erroneous idea that to God 'works' is a dirty word. This is totally false. While he condemns works done to earn salvation, and works done to impress others, our Lord enthusiastically *commends* righteous works done for the right reasons. . . . God created us to do good works, has a lifetime of good works for each of us to do and will reward us according to whether or not we do them. Indeed, Scripture ties God's reward-giving to his very character: 'God is not unjust; he will not forget your work and the love you have shown him as you have helped his people and continue to help them' (Heb. 6:10).

We should be interested in eternal rewards because they are the confirmation that our completed salvation was also a meaningful salvation. Rewards are God's way of saying, "You followed through. You discovered the reason I saved you and lived up to it. Nice going."

Rewards Demonstrate More than Love

If you've heard people say, "Forget all this talk about eternal rewards. We should serve Jesus just because we love him," I agree. We should serve Jesus because we love him, but as spiritual as those comments sound, they aren't very logical.

Suppose you want to build an apartment for your aging widowed mother on the back of your house so she'll be close to you and your family. You love your mother, and you want her to live her golden years in comfort and joy. But you're not a builder, and you aren't at all knowledgeable about construction. Nonetheless, for months you spend every spare minute framing and finishing the apartment. Then comes the day when she moves in. It's rather traumatic, because your dad and mom had lived so long in the house they had built with their own hands.

What eases the move is that she has pictures to hang and knickknacks to place around the apartment that will help her feel at home. When she pounds a nail in the wall and misses the stud, she asks, "Help me find that board behind the wall, so I can hang your father's picture." You begin pounding away, one hole after another, until the new wall looks like Swiss cheese. When your neighbor arrives and asks, "Didn't you set those studs sixteen inches on center?" your puzzled face answers his question.

You see, you built an apartment for your mother out of love, but you didn't follow the rules. You didn't pay attention to code. You just loved your mom so much, you wanted to serve her.

Some Christians are like that when it comes to serving the Lord. They love him so much, yet they don't stop to get directions or guidance from his "house plans" found in the Bible. They want to serve, but they don't know how, where, why, or when. Their service becomes haphazard, undependable, sometimes even useless.

Rewards demonstrate more than love. They demonstrate obedience, understanding, following the rules, and building a Christian life that's up to God's code. They are the Masterbuilder's "certificate of occupation" indicating that he approves of the way you have built your life. That's why you should think about your eternal rewards.

Rewards Provide Motivation

Loving Jesus is motivation for serving him. But God doesn't stop there. His gracious rewards are a strong and legitimate motivation for us to serve our Savior.

Jesus commands us to lay up treasures for ourselves in heaven (Matt. 6:20). He urges us to become "rich toward God" (Luke 12:21). It's a healthy ambition, a holy ambition. In fact, it's an ambition that, rather than fostering selfishness, frees us from selfishness because it motivates us to seek the pleasure and glory of God.

If we never think about rewards, or if we hold the foolish notion that we shouldn't think about rewards, we will fail to grasp God's motivation for our life. The only thing that will provide us with the motivation we need is the truth. If you really want to be motivated to serve the Lord, factor God's eternal rewards into your thinking, and you'll be more motivated than the football players competing on Super Bowl Sunday.

Paul demonstrates this kind of motivation in his counsel to the Corinthians who were having some trouble running the Christian race. He knew rewards were a key motivating factor in their spiritual growth (1 Cor. 3:1–3). He knew rewards would help them lay the right foundation and build the right building on it (1 Cor. 3:9–10). But the apostle outdid himself when he compared our heavenly rewards to the laurels won at athletic contests. He said, "Do you not know that in a race all the runners run, but only one receives the prize? So run that you may obtain it. Every athlete exercises self-control in all things. They do it to receive a perishable wreath, but we an imperishable" (1 Cor. 9:24–25).

Rewards should be important motivation to us because our Lord and his apostles made frequent appeal to them as such. Think about these examples:

Christ Jesus: "Beware of practicing your righteousness before other people in order to be seen by them, for then you will have no reward from your Father who is in heaven" (Matt. 6:1).

Paul: "Do you not know that in a race all the runners run, but only one receives the prize? So run that you may obtain it" (1 Cor. 9:24).

James: "Blessed is the man who remains steadfast under trial, for when he has stood the test he will receive the crown of life, which God has promised to those who love him" (James 1:12).

Peter: "And if you call on him as Father who judges impartially according to each one's deeds, conduct yourselves with fear throughout the time of your exile" (1 Peter 1:17).

John: "Watch yourselves, so that you may not lose what we have worked for, but may win a full reward" (2 John 8).

Abraham was the patriarch of faith. He was the patriarch because from him came the Hebrew nation. He was a man of faith; when an unseen God made promises for an uncertain future, Genesis 15:6 records, "And he believed the LORD, and he counted it to him as righteousness." Godly men of the Old Testament desired "a better country, that is, a heavenly one. Therefore God is not ashamed to be called their God, for he has prepared for them a city" (Heb. 11:16). That's the motivation of eternal reward.

Moses chose rather "to be mistreated with the people of God than to enjoy the fleeting pleasures of sin. He considered the reproach of Christ greater wealth than the treasures of Egypt, for he was looking to the reward" (Heb. 11:25–26). That's the motivation of eternal reward.

Rather than being ashamed of talking about rewards, the Bible writers often spoke of them as motivation for right living. If they were so interested in the subject, shouldn't we be interested, too?

Rewards Were God's Idea

Rewards are God's doing. They were his idea, not ours. God is the one who developed the rewards, determined the criteria for awarding them, and demonstrated his grace by providing them for faithful service. Rewards arise from the heart of God.

Another thing—rewards aren't about us; they're about pleasing him. They reflect God's gracious character more than they reflect our useful service. Thankfully, what it takes to earn eternal rewards—our motives, disciplines, and characteristics—all lead to a more intimate relationship with our heavenly Father. That's why he promises us rewards—they are incentives to know him better and gifts for serving him through knowing him.

Remember Jesus' words: "If anyone serves me, he must follow me; and where I am, there will my servant be also. If anyone serves me, the Father will honor him" (John 12:26). Honor from the Father was the Father's choice to compensate faithful service, not ours. So don't be ashamed to talk about eternal rewards; Jesus wasn't. Most of all, you take care of your service, and God will take care of your reward.

Remember, "without faith it is impossible to please him, for whoever would draw near to God must believe that he exists and that he rewards those who seek him" (Heb. 11:6). Focus on faith. Focus on pleasing him. Focus on drawing near to God. And remember, too, that he is the rewarder of those who do.

Fathers love to reward their children. They do it out of love. Don't rob God of the joy of being a rewarding heavenly Father because you tell him you don't care. You should care. It's okay to think about your heavenly reward. God does.

44

PART TWO

The Judgment Seat

The judgment seat of Christ has the potential either to bring a Christ-follower to his or her knees in terror or to cause them to stand and shout "glory!" How can one event evoke such a diverse response? Misunderstanding.

The judgment seat of Christ is the most important day in your future and an important subject often neglected in Christian literature. More than thirty-five years ago when I was a young college professor, a student came to me and asked a question about the judgment seat of Christ. I answered his question to his satisfaction, but not to mine. So I went to the college library to see what I could find on the subject. I found virtually nothing. Although the library had some theology books that included a paragraph on the crowns, almost nothing was written specifically on this subject.

Since that time several books have been written on the topic. I'm happy to add this to their number. But the question still remains: why do we Christ-followers not know more about the most important event in our future? The day that shapes so much of our eternity is a puzzle to so many. Why is that?

In this section we will answer questions about what the Bible means by the "judgment seat of Christ." We want to know now, while there's still time to labor for our reward.

4

WHAT EXACTLY IS A JUDGMENT SEAT?

"It ought to be the business of every day to prepare for our last day."—Matthew Henry

THE ENGLISH WORDS "judgment seat" well describe what the judgment seat of Christ is all about. It's the location where our final job review as Christians will take place. But to gain a better understanding, let's go back in history, stop to rest in front of a real judgment seat, and think about what happened there.

The image of a judgment seat came from the Greco-Roman world where judgment took place on a platform or tribunal from which a judge would hear and decide cases. There are two words in the New Testament that indicate a "judgment seat." The first, used in James 2:6 and 1 Corinthians 6:2, 4, is *kritērion*, which means the rule by which one judges or the place where judgment is pronounced. Our English word "criterion" is derived from this word: A form of the word *kritērion* is used three times in the Bible:

- **1 Corinthians 6:2**: "Do you not know that the saints will judge the world? And if the world is to be judged by you, are you incompetent to try [*kritēriōn*] trivial cases?"
- **1 Corinthians 6:4**: "So if you have such cases [*kritēria*], why do you lay them before those who have no standing in the church?"
- **James 2:6**: "But you have dishonored the poor man. Are not the rich the ones who oppress you, and the ones who drag you into court [*kritēria*]?"

A Raised Platform

A form of the second word, *bēma*, is more common. *Bēma* actually means "to step," "to stride," or "the space that a foot covers." It came to mean a raised platform mounted by steps. In ancient Greece, the *bēma* was a dais, a rostrum or raised platform from which judgments were announced.

A form of this word is found in a dozen verses in the New Testament. Once it is used in the context of a step or the space that a foot covers: Acts 7:5.

Twice a form of the word *bēma* refers to Pilate's judgment seat: Matthew 27:19 and John 19:13.

Once it is used of Herod's judgment seat: Acts 12:21.

When Paul stood before Gallio, the proconsul of Achaia, the Corinth a form of the word *bēma* is mentioned three times: Acts 18:12; Acts 18:16; and Acts 18:17.

The judgment seat of Porcius Festus, Roman governor of Judea, is referred to twice in Acts 25: Acts 25:6 and Acts 25:17.

Because Festus was an official of the Roman Empire, Paul refers to this judgment seat as Caesar's *bēma*: Acts 25:10.

Search any of the verses above and you will see that none of them refers to an athletic contest. They all refer to the tribunal or official seat of Greek and Roman judges where political orations or judicial decisions were announced. But don't think of the *bēma* as a judicial court where judges sat with black robes and a jury waited to issue a verdict. It wasn't. The judgment seat was where cases were made before a single judge, and his decisions were announced. Often the *bēma* was simply where orations were delivered to the crowd or public announcements were made.

The *Bēma* of Christ

The final two references to the judgment seat are specifically to the heavenly *bēma*: Romans 14:10 and 2 Corinthians 5:10.

If you visit Corinth today you can still see its *bēma*, a large, once elaborately decorated platform located on the edge of the agora, the ancient Greco-Roman marketplace. The platform was raised to allow crowds to hear the judgments as they were announced.

But Paul was aware of other such raised platforms where announcements were made. The *bēma* on which judges sat during athletic contests to observe the events and announce the victors undoubtedly came into play in Paul's reference to the *bēma* of Christ. Specifically well known to the apostle were the Isthmian games, which were held on alternate years to the Olympics in ancient Greece.

If you drive from Athens to Corinth today, you can see a huge oval-shaped field where the Isthmian games were held. In fact, you can still locate buried in the ground the stone used for starting blocks at the races. When the races were over, the victors would come to the *bēma* to be announced as winners and be awarded their prizes.

The Heavenly *Bēma*

The alert apostle Paul draws on his firsthand knowledge of the *bēma* at Caesarea, Corinth, Athens, etc., when he describes the judgment seat of Christ. There was a natural correlation between them.

In the Greek athletic games, victorious athletes appeared before the *bēma* to receive their laurel crown and hear the commendation of the judge. At the heavenly *bēma*, victorious Christians will appear before the *bēma* of Christ to receive their crowns and hear the "well done" commendation of their Judge. In the Greek and Roman tribunals, those who appeared before the judge were there to be scrutinized and hear the announcement of the judge.

At the heavenly *bēma*, we will also appear to be scrutinized and hear the announcement of the Judge. We will not stand before Christ's judgment seat to be judged on our guilt or innocence. That question was settled long ago at the cross of Calvary. There Jesus Christ made atonement for our sin with his own blood. The judgment seat of Christ is not to decide whether we are saved or lost, but to judge the true merit of our performance for the Lord. During our life of service we are being closely scrutinized as a contender for the faith. At the heavenly *bēma*, the rewarding Judge will announce his findings and pass out rewards for faithful service.

5

WHO ARE JUDGED AT THE JUDGMENT SEAT?

"We'll hardly get our feet out of time and into eternity than we'll bow our heads in shame and humiliation. We'll gaze on eternity and say, 'Look at all the riches there were in Jesus Christ, and I've come to the judgment seat almost a pauper."—A. W. Tozer

WHO WILL STAND before the judgment seat of Christ to receive the commendation of the Judge? The analogy with the *bēma* of Greece and Rome is still helpful. Greek athletes were rewarded, not for being athletes—all who entered the race or arena were athletes—but for their performance on the field or in the ring. So, too, we will be judged and rewarded for our performance as servants of the Lord.

At the heavenly *bēma*, only God's children will appear. Only those who have come to faith in Jesus Christ will be present, because this is not a judgment for everyone. This is a judgment for the church.

Every Scripture passage in the New Testament that relates to the *bēma* or to heavenly rewards pertains to born-again believers of the church:

- Romans 14:10–12
- 1 Corinthians 3:12–15
- 2 Corinthians 5:9–11
- 1 Thessalonians 2:19–20

- 1 Timothy 6:18–19
- Titus 2:12–14
- 1 John 2:28

The New Testament uses the word "church" to indicate that group of people who have repented of their sin and received Jesus' sacrifice at Calvary as payment for their sin. Thus "church," in the New Testament, does not apply to a building. It does not apply to a particular denomination or religious group in general. It refers only to those who have received Jesus as their Savior, regardless of where they are or to which denomination they belong.

Not all who claim to be Christians are really "Christ's ones," purchased from sin by his precious blood. Many people have the mistaken idea that if they are not Jewish, Muslim, Buddhist, or something else, they are automatically a Christian. But the Bible says there is nothing automatic about being a Christian. Only those saved from sin and set apart to a life pleasing to God are Christians and included in Christ's "church."

A Strong Relationship

The relationship between Jesus Christ and his church is both unique and blessed. A oneness between Christ and his church exists that is unparalleled in human history. The Bible uses several metaphors to describe this relationship. The church is a body of believers of which Christ is the Head (Eph. 1:22; 5:23; Col. 1:18). The church is a building made of living beings (the saints) of which Christ is the Foundation and Chief Cornerstone (1 Cor. 3:9; Eph. 2:19–22). The church is a branch that, in order to survive, must be rooted in Christ the Vine (John 15:5). And the church is the bride of whom Christ is the Bridegroom (Eph. 5:23).

With this close association and unity it is reasonable to expect that Christ and his church would live together in the same place. Bodies and heads are together; buildings and foundations are at the same site; brides and bridegrooms live together—why would not Christ and his church?

Presently, however, this is not the case. This doesn't mean Christ has abandoned his church or no longer loves those for whom he died. Quite the contrary; he loves us so much that he is currently preparing an eternal dwelling for us. His promise is, "[since] I go and prepare a place for you, I will come again, and will take you to myself, that where I am you may be also" (John 14:3). Jesus Christ will come back to remove his church before he exercises his wrath in judgment on the earth (1 Thess. 5:1–11). From that point on we will live forever with him.

Personal Pronouns

Since only servants of the Lord appear at this judgment seat, and since we cannot be the Lord's servants unless we are saved from sin, only those who are saved will stand before the righteous Judge at the heavenly *bēma*.

In those portions of Scripture dealing with the judgment seat, the first-person plural pronoun (we) occurs frequently. For example, in Paul's second letter to the Corinthians, he uses "we" no less than eighteen times in the first ten verses.[1] He is addressing "the church of God that is at Corinth, with all the saints who are in the whole of Achaia (southern Greece)." Both the words "church" and "saints" are terms reserved for believers, followers of Christ.

Paul could not possibly have included the unbeliever in the "we" of 2 Corinthians 5 for the following reasons: the unbeliever has no building from God (v. 1); he has not the guarantee of the Spirit (v. 5); he does not walk by faith (v. 7); he has no confidence in being present with the Lord upon death (v. 8); and he does not make it his aim to please the Lord (v. 9). Consequently, the person who is not a follower of Christ does not appear before the judgment seat of Christ (v. 10).

It is evident that those who are judged at the *bēma* of Christ belong there. This will be a judgment of the church, not of mankind in general.

Only those who qualify will be able to stand there, and we qualify solely through the death of Jesus Christ on our behalf. We will be judged for the things done in our bodies, whether good or bad. We will not be judged as sinners or even as sons. At the judgment seat of Christ we will be judged only as servants of the living God.

Won't Unbelievers Be Judged?

But what about those who have rejected Christ? Won't they be judged? Yes, but as mentioned in the introduction, they will appear before the great white throne judgment, pictured in the book of Revelation.

Here is the apostle John's description of what happens at the great white throne in Revelation 20:11–15:

> Then I saw a great white throne and him who was seated on it. From his presence earth and sky fled away, and no place was found for them. And I saw the dead, great and small, standing before the throne, and books were opened. Then another book was opened, which is the book of life. And the dead were judged by what was written in the books, according to what they had done. And the sea gave up the dead who were in it, Death and Hades gave up the dead who were in them, and they were judged, each one of them, according to what they had done. Then Death and Hades were thrown into the lake of fire. This is the second death, the lake of fire. And if anyone's name was not found written in the book of life, he was thrown into the lake of fire.

Does that sound like the same event as the judgment seat of Christ? Obviously not. When the book of life is opened, those standing before the great white throne will be shown that their name is not included. They have rejected God and his gospel. They have decided they didn't need Jesus as their Savior, and the absence of their names will prove they indeed belong at this solemn judgment.

Notice these who have not followed Christ will also be judged "according to what they had done." As was said before, there are degrees of punishment in hell just as there are degrees of reward in heaven. But the end result of the great white throne judgment will be that all who stand before this judgment bar of God will be condemned to the lake of fire. Anyone whose name is not found in the book of life is consigned to the lake of fire forever.

How different is the scene at the judgment seat of Christ. It leads to the blessedness of reward in heaven with God forever. It is clearly the Christian who will one day stand before the judgment seat. The world will have no more a part there than a non-athlete would have had before the *bēma* of ancient Corinth, begging to receive a laurel.

Make sure you're ready to stand at the right judgment.

6

WHO IS THE JUDGE?

"It is my happiness that I have served Him who never fails to reward His servants to the full extent of His promise."
—John Calvin

ANSWERING THE QUESTION, who is the Judge? is not rocket science. If the heavenly *bēma* is called the "judgment seat of Christ," shouldn't it be evident that the Judge is Jesus Christ? He is the most qualified person to discern if our service to God is acceptable, and the Father has charged Jesus with that responsibility.[1]

Judges are usually elected or appointed officials. The qualifications for this high office supersede simple party considerations. Most people want to know: "Is this the best man or woman for the job?" "Does he or she have good judgment?" and most importantly, "Is this a person of integrity?" Judges should be of high moral fiber and unquestionable character. They should be sympathetic and responsive to the needs of those they judge.

Qualifications to Be a Judge

These characteristics were foremost in the minds of the early Jews when electing a man to the Sanhedrin, the Supreme Court of

Judaism. It was a requirement that the Sanhedrinist should be married and probably a father as well. This, it was felt, would give him the proper sympathy for his fellow man so he would temper justice with mercy. Today a good judge is one whose character allows him or her to mete out justice with love and tenderness. A good judge cannot stay necessary punishment, but neither can a judge be unreasonably severe in assigning it.

If these requirements are recognized for a good judge in our society, should not the requirements for the Judge at the judgment seat of Christ at least meet or exceed them? The Judge sitting at the heavenly *bēma* must be one who is acquainted with the trials of men. He must be kind and compassionate, yet fair and just. In short, he must be better qualified than your average judge.

Actually, such a Judge should be God. He would be fair and accurate in discerning the validity of our service, and he would be entirely honorable when handing out rewards. By the same token, it would be ideal if this Judge were a human so he would be sympathetic and understanding toward the difficulties we have had in serving God. This would mean that the perfect Judge would be both God and man. But where would you find someone like that?

The Perfect Judge

That is exactly what Jesus Christ is—the perfect God-man. In keeping with God's commitment to justice and righteousness (Gen. 18:25; Job 8:3; Ps. 89:14), the Judge at the judgment seat is indeed the perfect Judge, Jesus Christ.

The Lord Jesus, who is God in the flesh, will certainly make honest and holy judgments when awarding rewards, because it is the essence of God to be honest and holy (John 14:6; Heb. 7:26). As a man, Jesus knows men (John 2:24–25). As a human being, he was tempted in all points like we are, yet he did not fall victim to sin (Heb. 4:15). He is sympathetic with, and understanding of, the problems we encounter in living a pleasing life to God.

The fact that the name of this heavenly *bēma* is the judgment seat of Christ (*bēmatos tou Christou*), leaves no doubt as to whom the Judge is. Of the two references to the judgment seat of Christ, the first (Rom. 14:10) is more literally translated "judgment seat of God." This is no problem, however, for Jesus Christ is God, and it would be entirely proper to refer to his *bēma* as the judgment seat of God. Paul is more specific in 2 Corinthians 5:10 when he mentions the same *bēma* as the "judgment seat of Christ." There can be no question that Paul is referring to the same judgment seat.

Jesus as Judge

Furthermore, there are a number of biblical references to Jesus as Judge. Jesus himself said, "All authority in heaven and on earth has been given to me" (Matt. 28:18). That power or authority includes the authority to judge all the people of the earth. Jesus will be a righteous and fair judge. The answer to the question, "Shall not the Judge of all the earth do what is just?" (Gen. 18:25) is, yes he will. Of course he will. How could we think otherwise?

Looking forward to the time of his departure, Paul thinks about the crown of righteousness "which the Lord, the righteous judge, will award to me" (2 Tim. 4:8). Peter says of Jesus that "he is the one appointed by God to be judge of the living and the dead" (Acts 10:42).

Luke records in Acts 17:31 that God has appointed a day in which he will judge the world in righteousness "by a man whom he has appointed." As we have noted, the only man qualified to be that Judge is Jesus Christ.

Here's an express statement of Scripture: "The Father judges no one, but has given all judgment to the Son" (John 5:22). It is quite evident, therefore, that we will be dealt with fairly at the judgment seat of Christ. Any reward that is earned and proven worthy will be awarded to us because of the very nature and integrity of the one who judges us, the Lord Jesus Christ.

7

WHEN WILL THE JUDGMENT TAKE PLACE?

"There are only two days on my calendar: Today and that Day." —*Martin Luther*

SINCE EVERYTHING WE ENJOY for all eternity is judged acceptable and awarded at the judgment seat of Christ, you wouldn't expect a fair God to allow us to go halfway through eternity before we began enjoying our rewards. I don't think he'll make us wait at all. It makes the most sense to believe the event of the heavenly *bēma* will take place soon after time gives way to eternity. The writer of Hebrews reminds us of this fact when he says, "It is appointed for man to die once, and after that comes judgment" (Heb. 9:27).

While we may not be able to pinpoint the time, perhaps we can determine a not-later-than date and a not-earlier-than date for the judgment seat. The Latin expressions for these two dates are *terminus ad quem* and *terminus a quo*. Just remember "not after" and "not before."

Terminus ad Quem

What is the absolute latest time the judgment seat could occur? Well, it must come before the marriage of the Bridegroom and his bride. As Christ's bride, we will be adorned with clean, fine, white linen, which the Bible says is the righteous deeds of the saints. Here are the apostle John's words in Revelation 19:6–8 describing this glorious scene:

> Then I heard what seemed to be the voice of a great multitude, like the roar of many waters and like the sound of mighty peals of thunder, crying out,
>
> 'Hallelujah!
> For the Lord our God
>   the Almighty reigns.
> Let us rejoice and exult
>   and give him the glory,
> for the marriage of the Lamb has come,
>   and his Bride has made herself ready;
> it was granted her to clothe herself
>   with fine linen, bright and pure'—
>
> for the fine linen is the righteous deeds of the saints.

Being dressed in the righteous deeds of the saints means that we will stand dressed in what, by the grace of God, we have been allowed to keep as a result of our works being deemed acceptable by the Lord Jesus. In order to determine what is acceptable, an evaluation of our life of service must occur first. That's the judgment seat of Christ, and so it must come before the marriage supper of the Lamb.

The marriage supper is at the beginning of the earthly kingdom of God. The celebration and jubilation of this wedding will usher the saints into the millennial kingdom (Rev. 20:6). Since the judgment seat must occur before the marriage supper, the *bēma* must be before the beginning of the millennium. That's the not-later-than date for the judgment seat of Christ.

Terminus a Quo

So, if the judgment seat cannot occur after the beginning of Christ's earthly rule during the millennium, what is the earliest time it could occur? This is the *terminus a quo*, the first point in time. Obviously, the judgment seat of Christ cannot take place before the rapture of the church, when the Lord shall "catch up" his bride to heaven (1 Thess. 4:13–18). Luke 14:14 makes it clear that followers of Christ will be rewarded at the resurrection of the just. Since the rapture involves the resurrection of the bodies of those Christ-followers who have died and the removal of those still living from the earth to heaven, the judgment seat cannot come before this. If we were to be judged before the rapture, conceivably there would be opportunity for service between judgment and rapture. This would mean some of our life and service would go untried and unrewarded. That would never do.

Thus, sometime between the rapture and the beginning of the millennium all Christians who are caught up to meet the Lord in the air must stand before the heavenly *bēma* and have their lives of service evaluated. It is the greatest event in our future. This day gives opportunity for us to be rewarded and, as we shall see later, one of those rewards relates specifically to continued and enhanced service in the kingdom of God.

What about Those Who Have Already Died?

If you are like me, you may have parents, grandparents, siblings, or children who came to faith in Christ and lived their lives for Christ. Their service for the Lord as we know it ended when their life ended. So what about them? Have those who predeceased us already appeared at the judgment seat of Christ?

No. In the Bible Jesus Christ is portrayed presently as being an intercessor, not a judge (Heb. 7:25; 1 Tim. 2:5). Those who have died in Christ are absent from the body and present with the Lord, but much of the information that relates to our eternal rewards relates to our bodies. To cast your crown at Jesus' feet takes hands. To hold a place of administration in his earthy kingdom, which is a genuine, real-time kingdom, will require a body. Second Corinthians 5:10 reminds us that at the heavenly *bēma* we will receive the things done in our bodies, and it doesn't seem likely that judgment and eternal reward would be done before those who have died in Christ were reunited with their resurrection bodies.

The Bible is very clear that Christ-followers who are yet living will not have an advantage over those whose lives have ended. Those who are "dead in Christ" (i.e. they trusted Christ as Savior during their lifetime but have since died) will be raised to join those of us still alive when Christ returns. That's the essence of Paul's teaching in 1 Thessalonians 4:13–18:

> But we do not want you to be uninformed, brothers, about those who are asleep, that you may not grieve as others do who have no hope. For since we believe that Jesus died and rose again, even so, through Jesus, God will bring with him those who have fallen asleep. For this we declare to you by a word from the Lord, that we who are alive, who are left until the coming of the Lord, will not precede those who have fallen asleep. For the Lord himself will descend from heaven with a cry of command, with the voice of an archangel, and with the sound of the trumpet of God. And the dead in Christ will rise first. Then we who are alive, who are left, will be caught up together with them in the clouds to meet the Lord in the air, and so we will always be with the Lord. Therefore encourage one another with these words.

All who make up the church, all who are Christ's bride, will stand before the judgment seat of Christ at the same time. So, Jesus has not yet entered the courtroom and ascended the steps of the *bēma*. He will not do so until he has retrieved to himself in heaven all those whose works are to be judged.

What the Scriptures Say

Most imposing is the list of New Testament references that indicates rewards are not given out until the Lord's return. The rewarding of the saints is spoken of in association with "that day," which refers to the glorious day when we will be gathered into Christ Jesus' arms:

- **1 Corinthians 4:5**: "Before the Lord comes. . . . Then each one will receive his commendation from God."
- **2 Timothy 4:8**: "Henceforth there is laid up for me the crown of righteousness, which the Lord, the righteous judge, will award to me on that Day. . . ."
- **Revelation 22:12**: "Behold, I am coming soon, bringing my recompense with me. . . ."

It is evident that rewards are not a present possession, and they are not awarded at the servant's death. They will be awarded only after the servant is judged, and that event occurs at the judgment seat of Christ.

The verses above demonstrate an emphasis on the future, the day in which the Lord will come. There are other Scripture passages that do the same:

- **Matthew 25:19**: "Now after a long time the master of those servants came and settled accounts with them."
- **Luke 14:14**: "You will be repaid at the resurrection of the just."
- **Philippians 2:16**: "I may be proud that I did not run in vain or labor in vain."
- **1 Thessalonians 2:19**: "For what is our hope or joy or crown of boasting before our Lord Jesus at his coming? Is it not you?"
- **1 Peter 5:4**: "And when the chief Shepherd appears, you will receive the unfading crown of glory."
- **1 John 2:28**: "And now, little children, abide in him, so that when he appears we may have confidence and not shrink from him in shame at his coming."

A simple reading of God's Word leads us to understand that we are still awaiting the day when we will stand before the heavenly *bēma* and the heavenly Judge will evaluate our works and our lives. The judgment for our sins is past; the judgment for our service is yet future.

Simultaneous Judgments

There is an interesting footnote to the timing of the judgment seat of Christ. It will occur simultaneously with the worst period the earth has ever seen or will ever see—the tribulation period.[1] Think about these two events together.

God has promised to keep us from the day of wrath (1 Thess. 5:9) because he has chosen us for salvation. Christians have been caught up to meet the Lord, but once we're gone, chaos will break out on the earth. This is the time of Jacob's trouble (Jer. 30:7). Satan hates Israel because this nation was God's channel to bring the Savior into the world. Satan, who has relentlessly persecuted Israel throughout her history, will intensify his persecution during the tribulation. In fact, his attacks on God's covenant people will become even more vicious when he realizes that the end of his long war against God is in sight.

Two judgments will take place simultaneously. One is a judgment of God's people, the church. The other is the judgment of God's people, Israel. One occurs at the heavenly *bēma*; the other occurs on earth. One occurs at the judgment seat of Christ; the other occurs during the tribulation period.

Now we await Christ's coming as a bride awaits the coming of her Bridegroom. The judgment seat cannot be long after the rapture, for the wedding is not long after the Bridegroom receives his bride. The events of the rapture and *bēma* occur in a very short space of time. There will be no anxious waiting for an examination. The Bridegroom will see to that at once, and we will enter into our marriage with him fully clothed in the garments of service that have withstood the trial by fire.

8

WHERE WILL
THE JUDGMENT SEAT BE?

"[The judgment seat] is not a declaration of gloom, but an assessment of worth, with the assignment of rewards to those who because of their faithfulness deserve them and a loss or withholding of rewards in the case of those who do not deserve them."—Philip Edgcombe Hughes

EVERYTHING HAS TO HAPPEN somewhere. The inauguration of the president of the United States takes place on the front steps of the Capitol in Washington, DC. Space exploration is guided by a team of highly skilled individuals at the Johnson Space Center in Houston. In 2012 the host city for the Games of the XXX Olympiad will be London.

Certainly the most important event in the future of the believer, with regard to what we enjoy for all eternity, is the judgment seat of Christ. Where will the *bēma* be? It has to be somewhere, and that place is in heaven.

Caught up from the Earth

If the time of the judgment seat of Christ must be immediately after Christ snatches away his church from this world and before our marriage to the Lamb (discussed in chapter 7), the place of judgment can scarcely be anywhere but heaven.

To his friends at Thessalonica, the apostle Paul describes the rapture of the church in hopeful language (1 Thess. 4:13–18). Paul's words imply the judgment seat of Christ cannot occur on earth because we are going to be swiftly removed from the earth before the *bēma* event. A judgment of the church that occurs after the rapture, therefore, cannot occur on the earth.

Paul refers to our removal from this world as our "blessed hope." Here's what the apostle says to Titus, one of the men he mentored in "things to come":

> For the grace of God has appeared, bringing salvation for all people,
> training us to renounce ungodliness and worldly passions, and
> to live self-controlled, upright, and godly lives in the present age,
> waiting for our blessed hope, the appearing of the glory of our great
> God and Savior Jesus Christ, who gave himself for us to redeem us
> from all lawlessness and to purify for himself a people for his own
> possession who are zealous for good works.

That's Titus 2:11–14. But this was not the first time Paul addressed the idea that we may be redeemed out of this lawless world without tasting death. Remember the apostle's words to the Corinthians: "Behold! I tell you a mystery. We shall not all sleep, but we shall all be changed, in a moment, in the twinkling of an eye, at the last trumpet. For the trumpet will sound, and the dead will be raised imperishable, and we shall be changed" (1 Cor. 15:51–52). If you begin reading in Genesis and read through the Pentateuch (the first five books of Moses), you will never encounter any teaching stating that it's possible we might go to heaven without dying. It just isn't there. In fact, you can read the whole Old Testament, and while you'll find a strong belief in bodily resurrection, you will never encounter the idea that you could enter eternity without dying.

What's more, read all four of the Gospels (Matthew, Mark, Luke, and John). They, too, are silent on this blessed hope. It's not until you get to 1 Corinthians 15 that you get a clue that the potential exists that we could be taken out of this earth to live forever with the Lord without experiencing the pain or sadness of dying. That's why Paul talks about the blessed hope being a mystery, a truth that has always existed but has never before been revealed.

The judgment seat of Christ cannot take place before this mysterious event. But it would be inconceivable that Jesus would hold a probative inquiry into your life "on the way up," so to speak. Our rapture will happen in the twinkling of an eye, and there's no need to get the judgment seat of Christ in before we reach heaven. So when Paul says that after we go to be with Christ we will forever be with our Savior and the *bēma* appointment will take place wherever the Judge is—and that's in heaven (Rev. 4:2).

Present with the Lord

Furthermore, 2 Corinthians 5:1–8 encourages us to face our own death with confidence because we know that "while we are at home in the body we are away from the Lord." With Paul, our desire is to "be away from the body and at home with the Lord." Death isn't the end; death is simply a transition from one life to another, from one place to another. For the believer, whether taken to Jesus by death or by living rapture, one thing is sure—we will most assuredly stand before him as our Judge and Rewarder. This event must occur in heaven, for judgment can only take place where the Judge and judged are.

The Bible indicates that after our translation from this earth we will live in heaven with our Savior (John 14:1–3). While we are destined for a new heaven and a new earth,[1] that's quite a ways down the road. Since the time of the judgment seat of Christ is immediately after the rapture, and the new heaven and new earth are a thousand years away, the only logical place for our judgment to occur is in God's present home—heaven.

It is an awesome thought that the rewards judged appropriate at the judgment seat will determine our possessions and standing for all eternity. That's a very long time. What is even more awesome is that the service we do now for the Lord will be the basis for that judgment at the heavenly *bēma*. This makes our present work for the Lord of the greatest human importance because when we are present with the Lord, all opportunity for service to earn rewards for eternity will cease forever. That's a sobering thought. We have all of eternity to enjoy what is judged acceptable at the judgment seat, but a very short time before he comes to earn those rewards. We'd all better get busy.

9

WHY WOULD GOD JUDGE ME? I THOUGHT HE LIKED ME

"We need not therefore be surprised if the Psalms and the Prophets are full of longing for judgment, and regard the announcement that 'judgment' is coming as good news."
—C. S. Lewis

WHY DOES GOD have to judge us? If we've earned a reward, he ought to just give it to us, right? Besides, if God likes us so much, why would he do this to us? Why is this most reflective event in our future even on God's calendar?

The judgment seat of Christ will happen because God does like you. Even more, he loves you (John 3:16). By nature, God is holy, just, and fair. Everything he does arises from his character and is in keeping with his character. The judgment seat is on God's calendar because of his character.

God cannot act contrary to who he is. Because he is holy, he cannot allow anything to exist in heaven that is unholy, including any service we perform in this life that is unacceptable. Because he is just, he cannot allow any acceptable deed we've done to languish unhonored. And because he

71

is fair, God cannot allow uncorrected impressions or misperceptions to continue throughout eternity; God must set the record straight. That's what the judgment seat of Christ does.[1]

As the apostle Paul notes, "We know that the judgment of God rightly falls on those who practice such things" (Rom. 2:2). Since God alone knows what is ultimately true because he is the source of ultimate truth, God alone is in a position to make a holy, just, and fair determination of our lives of service here on earth.

The Judgment of Others

Paul speaks of three types of judgment we all experience (1 Cor. 4:1–5). First, he says we all will be subjected to the judgment of other people. People make judgments about us all the time. Sometimes their perceptions are true and accurate; sometimes they are not. But because other people rarely possess all the facts, when it comes to importance, the judgment of other people is on the bottom rung of the ladder. That's why in verse 3 Paul says, "But with me it is a very small thing that I should be judged by you or by any human court."

The judgment we receive from others includes everything from those decisions handed down in a court of law to critical assessments made by neighbors or church members. We are all prone to make judgments. Everyone comes to conclusions about others based on what we see or hear. We all do it. But sometimes our judgments are just flat wrong, and we can do a lot of damage to others when we make judgments about them.

There are times, though, when the judgment of others is valuable, such as when your friends or family see things in you that you don't see yourself. But typically the judgment of others is often inferior to self-judgment, and it is always is inferior to God's judgment.

The Judgment of Ourselves

Paul also speaks of self-judgment. He says, "I do not even judge myself. For I am not aware of anything against myself, but I am not thereby acquitted . . ." (1 Cor. 4:3–4). If we can be honest with ourselves, self-judgment is better than judgment by others. We possess the facts, good and bad, that relate to our attitudes, our motives, and our actions.

Self-judgment occurs when we make a mental assessment of what we do and why we do it. For example, in the story of the prodigal son, the naïve younger son left his father and home. He wanted to run his own life his own way. He likely saw his father as restrictive and old-fashioned. But when reality hit him in the face, and he was completely tapped out and hungry, the son engaged in some mental self-assessment. He thought to himself, *You know, it wasn't as bad at home after all. Why, my father's hired servants have it better than I do. I've been so stupid; I need to go back to my father and see if he'll take me back* (see Luke 15:17–19).

Self-judgment is an examination of our behavior, our attitudes, and our motives. But even our own judgment is sometimes skewed either by a lack of understanding or by an unwillingness to admit the facts. Truth be told, it's easy to deceive ourselves. "If we say we have no sin, we deceive ourselves, and the truth is not in us" (1 John 1:8). That's why Paul did not even trust his own judgment in the important issue of how well he was doing in serving the Lord. He could let his conscience be his guide, but Paul knew better than to trust himself.

The Judgment of God

Paul finally speaks of our judgment by God himself. In 1 Corinthians 4:4 he says, "It is the Lord who judges me." God is not just our Creator, he is also our Judge. In some sense, every time we judge someone else's motives, we are presumptuously assuming a role that belongs to God alone.

You have to be struck with Paul's ranking of these three judgments. Paul did not place much value on the ability of others to judge his service. He didn't even place a great deal of stock in his own ability to judge himself. So his best option was to reserve the judgment of others and himself and let God do it rightly.

Why did the apostle value the divine judgment of God so much? First, God sees all things. Only God is aware of all the circumstances. He sees the struggles you have in serving Christ. He sees the good that could have come from your labors if only outside influences hadn't impacted them so adversely. Judgment is best left to God because only he sees everything that has happened.

Second, God knows all things—all things actual and all things potential. God knows your attitudes; he knows your motives; he knows your heart. "Man looks on the outward appearance, but the LORD looks on the heart" (1 Sam. 16:7). Man sees the deed but God sees the intention.

It's because God is in a much better position to discern why we do what we do and to assess the real outcome of what we have done that Paul concludes, "Therefore do not pronounce judgment before the time, before the Lord comes, who will bring to light the things now hidden in darkness and will disclose the purposes of the heart. Then each one will receive his commendation from God" (1 Cor. 4:5).

Enjoying God's Judgment

The purpose of the judgment seat of Christ is to discern the validity of our life of service to God. No one is in a better position to do that than God himself. His judgment will be fair and balanced. His judgment will be right.

For this reason, if you live rightly before God and the world, you should not fear the judgment seat of Christ. In fact, you should approach God's justice and his judgment with longing. This will be a great day for all who are unjustly judged today.

In the Old Testament the Hebrew word for judgment (*mishpat*) is not always used to convey condemnation; sometimes it is used in the sense of justice. For example, Psalm 37 offers encouraging admonitions and precious promises: "Trust in the LORD, and do good; dwell in the land and befriend faithfulness. Delight yourself in the LORD, and he will give you the desires of your heart. Commit your way to the LORD; trust in him, and he will act" (Ps. 37:3–5).

Too often that's where we stop—one verse too soon. The next verse says, "He will bring forth your righteousness as the light, and your justice as the noonday" (v. 6). The word translated justice is *mishpat*. The thought here is exactly the same as the judgment seat of Christ. God rewards those committed to him, but sometimes we have to wait for "noonday" when he will make all things right.

Psalm 96:12–13 says, "Let the field exult, and everything in it! Then shall all the trees of the forest sing for joy before the LORD, for he comes, for he comes to judge the earth. He will judge the world in righteousness, and the peoples in his faithfulness."

Why is God's creation so happy? Because the day of God's judgment is coming when all that is wrong will be made right, all that is misunderstood will be comprehended, and all that has been unjustly criticized will be appreciated. All who have lived obedient lives for God anticipate the judgment seat; we long for it, welcome it. It will mean justice.

If you feel you've ever been judged unjustly, you'll enjoy God's judgment. If you want rewards that come only from acceptable service, you'll enjoy God's judgment. If you don't trust how others judge you or how you judge yourself, you'll enjoy God's judgment. The judgment seat of Christ levels the playing field, and that may never have been the case before. God judges with righteousness and with truth, and that's a cause for rejoicing.

Why is God so willing to judge us? If, as the ancient Greek philosopher Socrates said, the unexamined life is not worth living, wouldn't it also be true that the unexamined life is not worth rewarding? God won't let you go through eternity with rewards that you didn't earn, nor will he keep from you that which rightfully belongs to you. An examination of your life of service is necessary to make sure everything is done right.

For the faithful Christian, God's judgment is a good thing. You should look forward to it.

10

DOES JUDGMENT MEAN I'LL BE CONDEMNED?

"He who provides for this life but takes no care for eternity is wise for a moment but a fool forever."—John Tillotson

IN THE TWENTY-FIRST CENTURY, we're generally interested in the bottom line. We want to know, "What's it all about?" and "What does it mean to me?" So when we face the judgment of God, does that imply that we will be condemned if we haven't been perfect? Is the judgment seat of Christ a place of condemnation?

The straight answer is no. The judgment seat of Christ is not a place of condemnation. Rather, it's a place of evaluation.

The condemnation (judgment) that is necessary because of your sins was paid in full by Jesus Christ at Calvary. When he suffered and died on the cross, he did all that God required to pay the penalty for your sin, and he did it so you wouldn't have to. He took the fall for you; he was condemned so you would not be. "For our sake he made him to be sin who knew no sin, so that in him we might become the righteousness of God" (2 Cor. 5:21). As the old gospel song says, "Jesus paid it all, all to him I owe. Sin had left a crimson stain, he washed it white as snow."

Here's a verse you'll want to put on the sticky side of your mind and never forget: "There is therefore now no condemnation [judgment] for those who are in Christ Jesus" (Rom. 8:1). Condemnation is past, it's over, and it's never coming back. It was poured out on Jesus Christ as he hung on the cross and endured all the condemnation for your sin. When you believe that Jesus is the Savior and ask him to be your Savior and to apply the work of his atonement on the cross to your account with God, condemnation is for you forever gone. It never becomes an issue again.

So the judgment at the judgment seat of Christ is not for the purpose of condemning you. It is for the purpose of evaluating your life of service to him. No condemnation; now evaluation.

When Paul said the purpose of judgment seat of Christ is "so that each one may receive what is due for what he has done in the body, whether good or evil" (2 Cor. 5:10), he did not use the usual words for bad. Rather, he used a word that does not imply ethical or moral evil, but rather a sense of good-for-nothingness or worthlessness. The judgment seat is where our works for the Lord will be closely scrutinized to see if they are valid or not, acceptable or not. The Judge is concerned with what sort of work we have done, what sort of life we have lived as a Christian servant.

Discernment, Not Condemnation

The purpose of the heavenly *bēma* is to evaluate us, not condemn us. This is an evaluation that leads Jesus, the righteous Judge, to discern what is pure and what is impure. First Corinthians 4:5 is very instructive in this regard: "Therefore do not pronounce judgment before the time, before the Lord comes, who will bring to light the things now hidden in darkness and will disclose the purposes of the heart. Then each one will receive his commendation from God."

The righteous Judge will see through all the things we have done in his name. Likely he will discern that many things we did, which we felt were very valuable, were actually quite worthless, perhaps because of the attitude with which we did them. He will sort out the works of our lives done through a pure motive and allow them to stand. At the same time, those things done with an improper motive will perish in the unquenchable fire (which we'll discuss later).

We all know some Christians who show little desire to serve their Lord wholeheartedly or fervently. And, we know others who serve God their entire lives with little or no recognition, rarely faltering in their dedication to the Master. Sometimes these people are even criticized for what they do, or their motivation is misjudged. This is unjust, but God is a God of justice. He will not allow injustice to prevail forever.

In the case of our service to the Lord, the heavenly *bēma* is the place where God will discern the quality of our work and reveal it to us. Jesus is simply there to evaluate what sort of service we've done for him. However, in what he discerns, there may be disappointment.

A contractor supposedly built a lovely house for a rich friend. But while building the house, the contractor threw his friendship to the wind in favor of cutting corners. Skimping in quality wherever it wouldn't be noticed, he put cheap material into the foundation, knowing that it would not be revealed for many years. The house looked imposing, but it was unsubstantial and unsafe.

You can image the contractor's disappointed surprise when he finished the house and the rich friend handed it over to him as a gift, with the one stipulation that the contractor had to live in it for the rest of his life! This foolish builder had inherited the fruit of his own unfaithfulness. Actually, in robbing his rich friend, he had robbed himself.

Sometimes that's true with us. If our present service for the Lord is faulty or insincere, we are not only robbing the Lord, but we are robbing ourselves of reward. The discerning fire of the judgment seat of Christ will test and verify our works.

Since Jesus will discern what kind of work our lives have produced, we need not worry about condemnation, but we should be concerned about loss. We can cheat ourselves out of much reward if we're not careful. In that sense, we condemn ourselves.

Keep Clear of Being a Castaway

Paul expressed concern about this in 1 Corinthians 9:27: "But I discipline my body and keep it under control, lest after preaching to others I myself should be disqualified." Paul was not worried about losing his salvation. He was worried that his service to the Lord would be found to be good for nothing.

The Greek word Paul chose for "disqualified" in 1 Corinthians 9:27 is the word castaway and indicates something that is tested for proof. If what is tested is found enduring, it is approved. If, however, when tested it is found to fail, it is disapproved or rejected. It becomes something you throw away. Paul does not want his labors to be in vain, to be rejected at the judgment seat of Christ. He doesn't want to be a castaway (the word the King James Bible translators chose). That's why he brings his body into subjection and does not allow his labors to be done in his own strength or for his own gain.

The apostle knows that the judgment seat of Christ is an evaluation, a discerning of quality. And Paul is eager that none of his service for the Lord be judged unworthy. When tested by fire, he wants his service to endure and be judged as acceptable. The only way to be sure that would happen was for Paul to live in the power of God's Spirit and not in the power of the flesh. That should be our attitude, too. It's the only acceptable attitude for rewardable service.

Don't let yourself become a castaway. Make certain now that all your service for the Lord is genuine and able to be judged and found approved.

Misconceptions Corrected

If you've been unjustly praised for service you have not performed or have performed for your own self-advancement, your work will be exposed for what it truly is and stripped away from you. If, on the other hand, you have labored in some dark, unnoticed corner of God's vineyard, where never any praise was heard nor thanks received, your service will finally be seen through the just eyes of the righteous Judge, who will recognize that you have done a valid work for him. At the judgment seat of Christ all misconceptions will be corrected because the heavenly *bēma* is all about discernment, not about condemnation.

Dr. Harry Ironside, beloved Bible teacher and for eighteen years pastor of the Moody Church in Chicago, summarized this thought as follows:

> Have you ever as a Christian stopped to think of what a solemn thing it will be when your life's work is ended, when all further opportunity for witnessing for Christ on earth will have gone by forever, when you stand in your glorified body before his judgment-seat, and he will go back over all the way you have come, and will give his own estimate of all your service, of everything you have attempted to do for him? Will he have to say at such a time, "You had a very wonderful opportunity to glorify Me, but you failed because you were so self-occupied, you were so much concerned about what people would think of you, instead of being concerned about pleasing Me; I will have to blot all that out, I cannot reward you for that, for there was too much self in that service"? And then he will point to something else, maybe something you had forgotten altogether, and he will say, "There! You thought you failed in that; didn't you? You really thought you blundered so dreadfully that your whole testimony amounted to nothing, but I was listening and observing, and I knew that in that hour of weakness your own desire was to glorify Me, and though nobody applauded you I took note of it and will reward you for it." What a joy it will be to receive his approval in that day. If we learn to live as Paul did with the judgment-seat of Christ before us, we will not be men-pleasers, but we will be a Christ-pleaser.[1]

In that day we will know what sort of work we have really done. Perhaps we will be shocked to see how little of our labors has been judged valid. Perhaps, too, we will receive rewards for something we thought was useless to the Lord.

Not Home Yet

Perhaps you can identify with the story of an old missionary couple who had been working in Africa for years and were returning to New York to retire. Henry C. Morrison and his wife had served the Lord in obscurity for forty years. Age had caught up with them, and it was time to come home to the United States. They had no retirement funds, no insurance; they were defeated, discouraged, and afraid. They wondered if anyone would even be there to greet them. But when the ship steamed into New York harbor, they couldn't believe their eyes. Thousands of people were there cheering. Bands were playing. There were signs, banners, and billboards everywhere saying, "Welcome Home." But the hoopla was not for the Morrisons. President Teddy Roosevelt was also a passenger on the ship. He was returning from a big game hunt in Africa. The signs, the cheering crowds, and the hoopla were all for him.

No one was there to meet this missionary couple. No one greeted them. No one noticed them. They quietly slipped off the ship and found a cheap flat on the East Side, hoping the next day to see what they could do to make a living in the city. That night the lack of appreciation got to Henry. He said to his wife, "I can't take this; God is not treating us fairly." His wife replied, "Why don't you go in the bedroom and tell that to the Lord?"

A short time later he came out of the bedroom with a completely different countenance. When his wife asked what happened, Morrison said, "The Lord settled it with me. I told him how bitter I was that the president received this tremendous homecoming, when no one met us as we returned home. It seemed as though the Lord put his hand on my shoulder and said, 'But Henry, you're not home yet!'"

I hope this is an encouragement to you. On that great evaluation day, at the judgment seat, the righteous Judge will discern what sort of work we have actually done. All service that crumbles in the trial by fire will prove worthless. But all service done through the constraining love of Christ will bring reward. Let's live our lives in light of this, knowing that Jesus Christ will be able to discern our actions, our motives, and our attitudes for service and will reward us accordingly.

It is at the judgment seat when we will fully appreciate the truth of David's words: "The LORD is merciful and gracious, slow to anger and abounding in steadfast love. He will not always chide, nor will he keep his anger forever. He does not deal with us according to our sins, nor repay us according to our iniquities. For as high as the heavens are above the earth, so great is his steadfast love toward those who fear him" (Ps. 103:8–11).

With condemnation behind us and eternity ahead of us, the judgment seat of Christ is not something to be dreaded. It's something to be anticipated.

11

WHAT IS THE PURPOSE
OF HEAVEN'S JUDGMENT SEAT?

*"God is not going to measure your intellect or ministry.
He is going to try your life with fire."—Leonard Ravenhill*

DO YOU KNOW the purpose of baseball's World Series? It depends
on who you ask. To the fans, it's to watch a game and enjoy a fall day. To
the players, it's to win the series and maybe feather their financial nest
while strengthening their bargaining power for the next season. To the
baseball commissioner, the purpose may be to garner more fans to insure
the future of America's pastime. And to the advertisers who pay to televise
the games? It's the bottom line. They want to sell a product.

But what's the real purpose of the game? While it may accomplish
all these goals for various interested parties, the purpose of playing the
World Series is to determine the best team in baseball.

That's the way it is with the judgment seat of Christ. While it is designed
to provide a forum to judge our life of service and reward us for eternity,
it accomplishes many other things as well. Let's investigate.

The *Bēma* Demonstrates the Presence of Salvation

In a valuable article, John Piper asks two significant questions about
the judgment seat of Christ. Piper ponders, "Is the aim of this judgment

85

to declare who is lost and who is saved, according to the works done in the body? Or is the aim of this judgment to declare the measure of your reward in the age to come according to the works done in the body?"[1]

The answer is "yes." The heavenly *bēma* both demonstrates that we are Christ-followers (for we would not be there if we weren't), and it demonstrates through the giving of rewards the measure of our service to our Master. If someone stopped you on the street and said, "How can I know you are a Christian?" would you say, "Just trust me when I tell you I am"? I don't think so; they would have no reason to trust you on your word alone. The apostle James says, "I will show you my faith by my works" (James 2:18).

The heavenly *bēma* is an appointment we must keep to be rewarded for our service to Christ, but just by being there it will also declare that we are servants of the Lord. We would not be invited to the judgment seat of Christ if we were not Christ-followers. If we had chosen to reject Christ and his gospel, our appointed judgment would be the great white throne judgment at the end of the millennial reign of Christ (Rev. 20:12–15). So, in some respect, the judgment seat of Christ confirms to all that we have followed the Lord Christ.

The heavenly *bēma* is the Supreme Court of judgment for the Christ-follower. It doesn't get any higher than that, and there are no courts of appeal beyond that. So, the judgment seat of Christ is the final public declaration that we have been people of faith, and that faith is proved by our works. Our service to the Lord will be the public evidence Jesus uses to demonstrate the varying degrees to which we have been obedient to walk in faith (cf. Rom. 12:3; 1Thess. 1:3; 2 Thess. 1:11). But the fact we are there demonstrates our faith in Christ as the only Savior of the world.

The *Bēma* Determines the Quality of Our Service

A second major function of the judgment seat of Christ is to evaluate and declare the genuine quality of our service to the Lord. First Corinthians 3:13 affirms that at the *bēma* each of us will be evaluated, and Christ the judge will determine the quality of our work. What sort of work did we do? Was it acceptable? Was it rewardable? That's the purpose of the *bēma* in heaven.

In a later chapter we will focus on the process by which Jesus judges whether our work for him is the quality of gold, silver, or precious stones, or whether our service turns out to have the lesser value of wood, hay, or stubble. Let's think more about how we can evaluate our service "on the fly" as we live today. Evaluation now can save a great deal of emptiness later.

Here are some questions you may wish to ask yourself about your service to the Lord. They address the kinds of issues that Jesus will take into account in determining the quality of your work.

Am I allowing the Holy Spirit to work through me, or am I just working my heart out to get as much done as I can? Working in the flesh profits us nothing (John 6:63). It is only as we are filled with the Holy Spirit (Eph. 5:18) that the quality of our work is *bēma*-acceptable quality. "Not by might, nor by power, but by my Spirit, says the LORD of hosts" (Zech. 4:6).

Is the fruit of my work for the Lord the fruit of the Spirit, or is it just personal fruit that is satisfying to me? "But the fruit of the Spirit is love, joy, peace, patience, kindness, goodness, faithfulness, gentleness, self-control: against such things there is no law" (Gal. 5:22–23). When Jesus said, "You will recognize them by their fruits" (Matt. 7:20), he did not mean that we would be personally fulfilled and happy about what we were doing, but that others would benefit from the character of our service.

Am I working for the Lord with the same intensity that he went to the cross for me? The Bible reminds us of the need to throw ourselves into whatever the Lord gives us to do and not work halfheartedly. Ecclesiastes 9:10 says, "Whatever your hand finds to do, do it with your might, for there is no work or thought or knowledge or wisdom in Sheol, to which you are going." The New Testament makes that even more specific for the Christ-follower: "Whatever you do, work heartily, as for the Lord and not for men, knowing that from the Lord you will receive the inheritance as your reward. You are serving the Lord Christ" (Col. 3:23).

Do a heart check today. Be tough on yourself. Examine all you do for the Lord, and ask the right questions to ensure the quality of your service is not something you will be ashamed of one day.

The *Bēma* Determines the Distinctive Rewards We Receive

The heavenly *bēma* will do more than just determine the quality of our service and rewards; it will also pair rewards to service. Both Paul and Jesus taught that those who follow Christ in obedience would receive differing rewards according to the degree that their faith expressed itself in loving acts of service. For example, in 1 Corinthians 3:8 Paul says, "He who plants and he who waters are one, and each will receive his wages according to his labor." Again in Ephesians 6:8 the apostle promises, "Whatever good anyone does, this he will receive back from the Lord."

If Christ gives to the church a variety of offices (Eph. 4:11–12) and a diversity of gifts (1 Cor. 12:4) for the work of the ministry, isn't it logical that this same diversity carries through in the rewards he gives for faithfully exercising these offices and gifts in various ministries? As head of the church he and he alone determines who receives which gift (1 Cor. 12:11), so as the judge at the judgment seat he and he alone determines what rewards we receive based on how we engaged those gifts.

Later in this book we will answer the question about the various kinds of rewards that will be awarded at the heavenly *bēma*. The distinctiveness of each reward reflects the distinctiveness of each servant, each spiritual gift, and each degree of effectiveness in exercising those gifts.

The *Bēma* Determines the Degree of Rewards We Receive

Finally, there is more to our heavenly rewards than distinctive qualities. The Quantity of rewards will also be determined at the *bēma* of Christ. Isn't this what the parable of the minas (or pounds) in Luke 19:12–27 teaches? Jesus compares his going to heaven and returning to a nobleman who, before going away, gave to each of his ten servants one mina to invest for him while he was gone.[2] They were to invest the mina so that the nobleman's estate would advance during his absence. When the nobleman returned, one servant had invested so wisely that he turned his mina into ten. He traded well, and the nobleman said that, as a reward, the servant would have authority over ten cities. Another servant turned his mina into five. The nobleman was pleased with him, too, and rewarded his efforts with authority over five cities. But another servant kept his mina and did nothing with it. To this one the nobleman said, "I will condemn you with your own words, you wicked servant!" And he took the one mina from him.

Jesus' parable teaches exactly what Paul taught: just as there are distinctive rewards that correspond to distinctive service, there are varying quantities of reward for the faithfulness of our lives. The judgment seat of Christ determines both the quality and quantity of our heavenly reward.

It should be becoming more evident that for all who are faithfully serving the Lord today, the judgment seat of Christ is something to be welcomed, not feared. Just thinking about it ought to get you up every morning.

PART THREE

Our Performance Evaluation

Performance evaluations are good things. The ministry I serve, Back to the Bible International, has used employee performance reviews for many years as a way to evaluate and measure our employees' on-the-job performance against our performance expectations. This is done to identify training needs and establish a mechanism for employee growth and development. Job reviews also encourage periodic and structured communication between supervisors and employees about their tasks, and they document a defendable rationale for decisions involving promotions, demotions, career development, terminations, salary increases, etc. Virtually all organizations in the private sector use some form of performance evaluation today. Supporters of nonprofit ministries expect top performance for their investment.

There are four primary types of employee performance evaluations. Peer-to-peer evaluation is popular today. This requires employees at the same level to evaluate each other. In 360-degree performance reviews, many different types of people are consulted about an employee's performance, including customers, suppliers, etc. With self-assessment reviews employees rate their own performance. Since this can be quite subjective, it is often used in conjunction with the final job review technique—the top-down employee performance evaluation, where the boss does the evaluation and rewards the employee according to his or her findings.

While there is evidence of each of these kinds of job reviews in the Christian's life, there is no question that the judgment seat of Christ is of this final type of performance evaluation. It is definitely top-down, as we'll see in the following chapters.

12

IS THE EVALUATION UNIVERSAL?

"Whatever this judgment seat is, we shall all stand before it. This scripture admits of no question at this point."
—L. Sale-Harrison

PREVIOUSLY WE HAVE been interested in the participants and physical setting of the heavenly courtroom. Once aware that Jesus Christ is the righteous Judge, and as Christ-followers we are the judged, it is only natural for us to wonder about the actual process of judgment at the *bēma* of Christ.

We are certain this judgment will come. Many of the Gospel parables teach that on the appointed day the Master will require his servants to give an account of their lives of service to him (Matt. 18:23; 25:19; Luke 16:2). Jesus promised rewards to his disciples (Matt. 5:3–12; Mark 9:41; 10:30). Judgment, in the form of evaluation, and the gain or loss of rewards are certain. The question is, what will that evaluation be like?

Universal and Exclusive

Since those judged at the judgment seat of Christ are only those who have expressed faith in Jesus Christ as Savior, it is safe to say that the appraisal of works at the heavenly *bēma* is both universal and exclusive. It is universal to all who have been born again by the Spirit of God and exclusive of all others. All believers will be present for this evaluation, and only believers.

Romans 14:10–12 declares, "Why do you pass judgment on your brother? Or you, why do you despise your brother? For we will all stand before the judgment seat of God; for it is written, 'As I live, says the Lord, every knee shall bow to me, and every tongue shall confess to God.' So then each of us will give an account of himself to God."

As if the Roman believers would not understand the universality of the believer's evaluation, Paul emphasizes, "We will *all* stand before the judgment seat of God" and "*each* of us will give account of himself to God." There was no doubt in Paul's mind. As the servants in the Lord's parables had to stand before their masters, so, too, every believer must stand before God and give account of his life and deeds. If you are a genuine Christ-follower, you have a divine appointment at the judgment seat of Christ. No Christian is excluded, regardless of how weak or strong his Christian life was.

All Must Appear

Paul picks up this same theme in 2 Corinthians 5. This phenomenal passage speaks of future hope and the believer's present purpose. The apostle compares the realities of his present suffering, which were significant (see 2 Cor. 11:16–33), to the promise of an "eternal weight of glory," which is even more significant (2 Cor. 4:17). He speaks of a day when he will receive a new body, "a house not made with hands, eternal in the heavens" (2 Cor. 5:1). For now, however, Paul knows painfully well that he is still in his body, aging and aching and, for the sake of the gospel, withstanding tortures that would do in a man half his age. The promise of heaven is someday for the Christ-follower, but the pain of earth is today. "So whether we are at home or away, we make it our aim to please him. For we must all appear before the judgment seat of Christ, so that each one may receive what is due for what he has done in the body, whether good or evil" (2 Cor. 5:9–10).

Paul uses the language of family when he says "we" must appear or be made manifest. The "we" excludes any who do not belong to the family and includes all who do. Everyone who has been washed clean in the blood of the Lamb will stand before him as a servant before his Master and will give account of his life of service to the Lord.

And who will do this? All who have followed Christ as their Lord. The deacon who taught your Sunday school class will be there. The college student whose life was snuffed out by a crazed gunman at Virginia Tech University will be there. The person who led you to the Lord will be there. Paul will be there and so will Peter and John. Martin and Katharina Luther will be there. So will John and Charles Wesley. The known and the unknown. The famous and the forgotten. All who have trusted Christ as their Savior must appear before their Savior as their Judge at the judgment seat of Christ. It should be quite a company.

If you are a Christian today, you won't miss this appointment. The honor of your presence is not requested, it is commanded. But then again, who would want to miss this?

13

IS THE EVALUATION NECESSARY?

"Though the mills of God grind slowly, Yet they grind exceedingly small; Though with patience He stands waiting, with exactness He grinds all."—Friedrich von Logau

WILLIAM COWPER WROTE, "God moves in a mysterious way, his wonders to perform." This, however, does not mean that God is illogical. The mystery of his movements may be a mystery only to us. We may not completely see the logic in God's saving men and women who have rebelled against him, but we can certainly see the logic in our separation and estrangement from God because of our sin.

So let's take logic one step further. If we must all stand before the judgment bar at which Christ evaluates us, is there some kind of logic behind this? Is the whole concept of the heavenly *bēma* just a motivational straw man, or does it stand the tests of logic, grammar, and more?

The Logical Conclusion

Maybe one of your many early morning classes in college was Philosophy. For me, a lot that I heard in philosophy class flew right over my head. It wasn't my professor's fault; he was a gem. My philosophy professor was an Episcopal priest. I can still see him riding to class in his white collar with his clerical robes flowing off the back of his Harley. Of the many things I remember from his class, the use of a syllogism stands at the front of my mind. A syllogism is a contrast of one premise or simple statement with a second premise or statement, resulting in a conclusion. Even if you never had any classes in logic, you'll be able to follow this syllogism:

> **Major Premise:** God is holy and can dwell only in a holy environment (Lev. 20:7; Deut. 26:15).
>
> **Minor Premise:** Man is unholy and can dwell only in an unholy environment (Rom. 3:10, 23; Isa. 6:5).
>
> **Conclusion:** God and man cannot dwell together (Isa. 55:8–9; Ps. 115:16).

That's Philosophy 101. If it is true that God is holy, and to live in an unholy environment would completely destroy his holiness, and if it is likewise true that mankind is unholy, and to live in a holy environment would only defile that environment, then the only logical conclusion is that God and man cannot live together unless something changes. That's why Christ Jesus came to die—to pay the penalty for our sins. He came to make the unholy holy in God's sight, to make it possible for us to live in heaven with him.

We were created in God's image (Gen. 1:27), and we walked with God (Gen. 3:8), but because of our sin, we became separated from his holiness and from his presence (Gen. 3:24). Jesus Christ came to bridge the gap between holy God and unholy man. He made it possible for us to live again with God (John 14:3). It's because of his death that we'll be able to enter heaven, but we can't take anything unholy with us. Since we may not have done some things in our life as we should have, we need to be examined before we embark on an eternity in God's holy presence. That's what the heavenly *bēma* is all about.

Can you handle another syllogism? Try this one on for size:

> **Major premise:** A holy God can reward only service done in righteousness and faith (Matt. 6:1; Heb. 11:6).

Minor premise: Not all of our service for God is done in righteousness and faith (Matt. 6:2, 5, 16; John 18:10–11).

Conclusion: A holy God cannot reward all of our service (Matt. 25:26–28; Mark 10:13–16).

God's holiness is complete, not partial. Being holy is like being perfect; you cannot be mostly perfect—either you're perfect or you're not. Either you're holy or you're not. A holy God cannot possibly reward unholy service done for him. The only logical conclusion is there has to be a judgment day, one that casts out everything that is unacceptable, before we are presented faultless to God. We enter heaven carrying some stuff with us that was done in our own strength. Everything done in the flesh has to be discarded to preserve the integrity of everything done in the Spirit. This is why the judgment seat of Christ is necessary.

The Grammatical Conclusion

But there's an even stronger argument for the necessity of the Lord evaluating our life of service. The actual words of Scripture make it conclusive that each of us must present ourselves at the judgment seat of Christ.

Paul reminds us, "For we must all appear before the judgment seat of Christ" (2 Cor. 5:10). His language is firm in the original Greek. Grammatically, the main verb of Paul's statement does not emphatically indicate that judgment is necessary. But it doesn't have to, because the main verb is accompanied by an impersonal verb *(dei)* that is always used to denote a strong compulsion or necessity. A simple rendering of the word is "must."

This is frequently used in Scripture to show necessity. Here are some examples:

- **Mark 8:31:** "And he began to teach them that the Son of Man *must* suffer many things and be rejected by the elders and the chief priests and the scribes and be killed, and after three days rise again."

- **John 3:7, 14**: "Do not marvel that I said to you, You *must* be born again. . . . And as Moses lifted up the serpent in the wilderness, so *must* the Son of Man be lifted up."
- **1 Corinthians 15:53**: "For this perishable body *must* put on the imperishable, and this mortal body *must* put on immortality."
- **1 Timothy 3:2, 7**: "An overseer *must* be above reproach. . . . Moreover, he *must* be well thought of by outsiders. . . ."
- **Hebrews 11:6**: "And without faith it is impossible to please him, for whoever would draw near to God *must* believe that he exists and that he rewards those who seek him."

Each event mentioned in the verses will come to pass because it must come to pass. Paul literally tells us, "It is necessary that we all be revealed before the judgment seat of Christ." There is no doubt.

Furthermore, we are assured that "we will all *stand* before the judgment seat of God" (Rom. 14:10) and that "each of us will *give an account* of himself to God" (Rom. 14:12). Both of these verbs denote that nothing will prohibit the evaluation of our deeds.

Standing before the *bēma* of Christ is an event that is not only universal in nature for all believers, but is also absolutely necessary for all who follow Christ. It's necessary that our service be evaluated because of God's holiness and justice. All believers must stand before Jesus Christ the Judge.

14

IS THE EVALUATION PRIVATE?

"The greatest thought that has ever entered my mind is that one day I will have to stand before a holy God and give an account of my life."—Daniel Webster

YOU AND I LIVE in a day when security is a high priority. As a result, many public places have become saturated with personal surveillance devices, closed-circuit televisions, and other sophisticated technologies that may well end privacy as we have known it. Facial recognition technology is being widely used. It you attend a football (soccer) match at The City of Manchester Stadium, your face will be photographed and image stored in a collection data device. The same is true on London's streets and at Heathrow airport. Germany started issuing biometric passports in 2005 using the same facial recognition technology. The U.S. Department of Homeland Security has spent millions of dollars on "smart" cameras that attempt to identify people based on their facial images.

All of this has increased our concerns about personal privacy. If you look at the bottom of most websites, you will see the words "Privacy Policy." This policy exists to inform you, the user, of the procedures that organization uses to collect data, how it is and is not used, and whether the organization shares that data with others. It's your assurance that when you click on a site, you are not allowing others to know things about you they have no business knowing.

The privacy issue carries over to our questions about the judgment seat of Christ. People ask: "Is everybody in heaven going to know all the things I've done? Will my life be flashed onto a huge screen for everyone to see? Are my friends and family going to know what I did in life that embarrasses me?" Let's face it. Anyone who is serious about the heavenly *bēma* is serious about this question. So what's the answer?

Our Service Record Will Be Visible

There is no question that our life of service for the Lord will be made visible at the judgment seat. Again the key verse is 2 Corinthians 5:10: "For we must all appear before the judgment seat of Christ, so that each one may receive what is due for what he has done in the body, whether good or evil."

In the beginning of this verse, the principal verb is "appear." There is more to this word than first meets the eye.

The word "appear" does not simply mean to "show up." We will not just put in an appearance at the judgment seat. This word more strictly means "made visible" or "to be clearly seen and explicitly discerned." When as a servant we stand before our Master, our lives of service will be totally revealed. Since the word is passive, we understand that we are not revealing ourselves, but he is revealing us. We are revealed not only to the Judge, but we are revealed to ourselves as well. Suddenly, perhaps for the first time, we will truly see what our life of service was like.

In this key verse, we gain deeper insight into the actual evaluation of our service. The verse says, "For *we* must all appear." Notice it did not say our works or our service must appear before the Lord, but "we" must appear before him. This is more personal. As individuals we are revealed in that heavenly courtroom.

There is an inseparable link between our service for the Lord and our life in the Lord. As a matter of fact, our service is our life, the deeds done in our body. Not only will what we have done for him be judged, but also what we are. We are presenting for judgment and reward what the Lord has been allowed to do with our life. Our motives for service, our capabilities for service, our desire for service, and our service itself are all wrapped up in one package that we will present for evaluation. This package is our life. At the *bēma*, the entire scope of our Christian life and service will be revealed.

The Revealing Day

First Corinthians 3:13 adds depth to our understanding of the visibility of this heavenly evaluation: "Each one's work will become manifest, for the Day will disclose it, because it will be revealed by fire, and the fire will test what sort of work each one has done."

Bear in mind the word "work" here, and implied in Romans 14:12 and elsewhere, represents the totality of our Christian life as well as our service. In this verse we learn that "the Day" will reveal our life. What is this day when our lives will be made transparent so that nothing is hidden?

Paul must be referring to a day he mentioned previously in this letter, in which he advises that we "wait for the revealing of our Lord Jesus Christ, who will sustain you to the end, guiltless in the day of our Lord Jesus Christ" (1 Corinthians 1:7–8). When Jesus comes to take his bride away, he will usher us directly to the heavenly *bēma* and will judge our lives according to what we have allowed the Lord to do with them. That is the day in which the Lord "will bring to light the things now hidden in darkness and will disclose the purposes of the heart" (1 Cor. 4:5). It is in that day that "God judges the secrets of men by Christ Jesus" (Rom. 2:16).

The implication is clear. On that day we will have our lives made visible before Jesus Christ our righteous Judge, and truly "all are naked and exposed to the eyes of him to whom we must give account" (Heb. 4:13). There shall be nothing hidden, as the verbs "manifest" and "disclose" indicate (1 Cor. 3:13).

Just as day brings light from the sun to reveal the hidden things of darkness, so will that day bring light from the Son to reveal the hidden things of darkness done in our bodies. However, many hidden things that are good will be revealed as well. Many services performed that went unnoticed will be seen. This will be a total revelation of our life and service to the Lord. It will be both a day of vindication and a day of disappointment.

The Evaluation Is Private

Although as believers our lives will become an open book on that day, and everything we have done in our body, both good and bad, will be revealed, I believe our judgment will remain a private matter. There will be no giant screen revealing to everyone the dirty laundry of our life. There is no public record read aloud. This is between the Judge and us.

Also, we will not be judged *en masse* or by groups or classes, but we will be judged as individual servants. Jesus the Judge will personally evaluate our life of service and reward us accordingly. This is an evaluation, not a circus. I believe this for several reasons.

First, although the Bible does not specifically state that we will stand one-by-one before the righteous Judge, many verses give that distinct impression. For example, Romans 14:12 says, "Each of us will give an account of himself to God." Our account deals with our life of service, and it's of private concern to Jesus our Judge. "For the Son of Man is going to come with his angels in the glory of his Father, and then he will repay each person according to what he has done" (Matt. 16:27). "For we must all appear before the judgment seat of Christ, so that each one may receive what is due for what he has done in the body, whether good or evil" (2 Cor. 5:10).

God Is Interested in Individuals

Second, God is very interested in the individual. He has already set a precedent. Many books of the Bible center around one person (e.g., Ruth, Job, Philemon, etc.). The Lord speaks to Satan directly and inquires of one of his children by name: "Have you considered my servant Job, that there is none like him on the earth?" (Job 1:8). The psalmist tells us,

O LORD, you have searched me and known me!
You know when I sit down and when I rise up;
    you discern my thoughts from afar.
You search out my path and my lying down
    and are acquainted with all my ways.
Even before a word in on my tongue,
    behold, O LORD, you know it altogether. (Ps. 139:1–4)

The Lord is so interested in the individual that "the hairs of your head are all numbered" (Matt. 10:30). All of Jesus' disciples, even Peter and Andrew who were found together, were called individually and personally (Matt. 4:18–22; see also 9:9). Jesus spoke frequently to people, often calling them by name, such as Peter (John 21:15–17); Zacchaeus (Luke 19:5); and Lazarus (John 11:43–44). The individual judgment of believers at the heavenly *bēma* is a personal matter between servant and Master, between creature and Creator, between the judged and the Judge. Because Jesus Christ has dealt with personal matters in a personal way in the past, we should expect that the matter of such private consequence as judging the stewardship of our lives would be a personal and private matter as well.

Besides, a private evaluation of our life and work is only natural. It is really nobody else's business what we have done for the Lord or why we have done it. This is a matter that concerns just you and your Judge (see John 21:20–23).

But if Jesus judges us privately, individually, and personally, how long must it take him to judge every servant who stands before him? You can see the process lasting more than the seven years of the tribulation. But the judgment seat of Christ need not cover a great expanse of time, for the Judge is the God who knows everything. If humans like you and me can multitask, don't you think the Judge of all the earth will have the ability to judge us individually, privately, and simultaneously?

At the heavenly *bēma*, you won't be concerned about what others think anyway. The focus will be on your life of service for the Judge. If Christ can see what went on in your life and why you did the things you did, no one else matters.

15

IS THERE REAL FIRE AT THE EVALUATION?

"All will be in heaven, but the differences will be eternal. We may be sure that the consequences of our character will survive the grave and that we shall face those consequences at the Judgment Seat of Christ." —Donald Gray Barnhouse

I WAS BORN and raised in a small steel town in western Pennsylvania. Almost every worker was employed by one of the large steel companies. My father-in-law was a crane man over the open hearth. During one of my summers home from college, I, too, became a "steel man" working in one of the mills as a summer job. It was quite a learning experience for me. Watching my colleagues work with liquid steel demonstrated the power humans have over the elements by simply applying fire to them.

High above the floor a giant crane carried the huge ladle of liquid steel from the blast furnaces and poured it into the waiting mold. These furnaces produced such intense heat that periodically the bricks that lined the inside had to be replaced because the heat caused them to crumble. As a matter of fact, just about everything that entered that furnace crumbled because of the intense heat.

Of course, the use of fire for melting and purifying purposes has been around for a long time. King Solomon built smelting plants at a city called Ezion-Geber, on the tip of the Gulf of Aqaba in southern Israel. The prevailing north winds caused a natural draft for his blast furnaces. Because the area of southern Palestine is rich in mineral wealth, especially copper, Solomon became the "copper magnate" of the world through his own ingenuity and by the grace of God.

Paul traveled through many of the industrial sections of Palestine and Asia Minor. He obviously was well acquainted with the refining qualities of fire. Probably he had this in the back of his mind when he wrote 1 Corinthians 3:13: "Each one's work will become manifest, for the Day will disclose it, because it will be revealed by fire, and the fire will test what sort of work each one has done."

The Refining Fire

It is important to understand that in 1 Corinthians Paul was not speaking of fire in a purgatorial or punishment sense. This is not an avenging fire but a refining fire. It does not burn people; it tests their lives. It is not disciplinary in character; it is discerning. This fire is not a form of torture in a nether world. It is an instantaneous fire that will disclose immediately "if the work that anyone has built on the foundation survives" (1 Cor. 3:14).

But Dr. Erwin Lutzer, pastor of the Moody Church in Chicago, asks, "Why do our works have to be subjected to the flames?" He then answers, "The natural eye cannot easily tell the difference between these building materials. Not even Paul was confident that he could always separate junk from gems. From our perspective, a believer might have nothing but an impressive pile of combustible material; but when torched, nuggets of gold might be found embedded in the straw. Conversely, what we thought was a gold brick of some notable saint might just be the end of a wooden beam. Only the fire can separate the real from the fake."[1]

This fire takes place on "the Day" that reveals our work, the day of evaluation at the heavenly *bēma*. Paul was speaking of a fire that will separate the destructible from the indestructible, the unacceptable from the acceptable, and the inferior from the praiseworthy. This fire is suggestive of what happens when something unholy comes into contact with the holiness of God.

Frequently in Scripture God is associated with fire. Often he appears to men in fire:

- **Exodus 3:2**: "And the angel of the LORD appeared to him [Moses] in a flame of fire out of the midst of a bush. He looked, and behold, the bush was burning, yet it was not consumed."
- **Exodus 13:21**: "And the LORD went before them [the Israelites] by day in a pillar of cloud to lead them along the way, and by night in a pillar of fire to give them light, that they might travel by day and by night."
- **Ezekiel 1:4**: "As I looked, behold, a stormy wind came out of the north, and a great cloud, with brightness around it, and fire flashing forth continually, and in the midst of the fire, as it were gleaming metal."

God is even referred to being like "a refiner's fire" (Mal. 3:2). Also, God's judgment is associated with fire:

- **Genesis 19:24**: "Then the LORD rained on Sodom and Gomorrah sulfur and fire from the LORD out of heaven."
- **Leviticus 10:1–2**: "Now Nadab and Abihu, the sons of Aaron, each took his censer and put fire in it and laid incense on it and offered unauthorized fire before the LORD, which he had not commanded them. And fire came out from before the LORD and consumed them, and they died before the LORD."
- **Numbers 11:1–3**: "And the people complained in the hearing of the LORD about their misfortunes, and when the LORD heard it, his anger was kindled, and the fire of the LORD burned among them and consumed some outlying parts of the camp. Then the people cried out to Moses, and Moses prayed to the LORD, and the fire died down. So the name of that place was called Taberah, because the fire of the LORD burned among them."

Particularly, fire is associated with the holiness of God. Holiness is the opposite of impurity, and where God is present, holiness is present. At the heavenly *bēma* God is present in the person of the Judge, Jesus Christ. Thus the trial by fire that our lives and works must endure may possibly be the simple presence of the Holy God in judgment. It is not necessary to assume that this is a literal fire. Literal fire is not needed because tangible material isn't being tested, but rather it's our very lives and what has been done with them. It may be that the glorious presence of our holy Judge will be enough to show our lives and service for what they really are.

Imagine how useless those things we have done with selfish motives will appear when they are exposed to the presence of God's holiness. Everything not done for his honor and glory will "melt" into insignificance and shame.

The Blazing Gaze

Revelation 1:14 describes Jesus Christ in this way: "The hairs of his head were white, like white wool, like snow. His eyes were like a flame of fire." Revelation 2:18 describes him as "the Son of God, who has eyes like a flame of fire." Is it possible that the fiery trial of our works will be accomplished simply through the blazing gaze of the Master on our life of service? Certainly he will be able to see through any service we have rendered to gain self-acclaim. His gaze will penetrate any work we have done out of impure motives, and his judgment will follow.

Likewise, his gaze will certify as pure any work that has been done faithfully and properly. The holiness of his presence and his scrutinizing look at our lives, with eyes "like a flame of fire," seem to be all that is necessary to burn up any unjust work or any glory-seeking service. The holy Judge will single-handedly and instantaneously be able to discern the true motive for our service and will melt away anything that smacks of insincerity or impurity. Likewise, he will reward that which stands the test of the refiner's fire.

Whatever this fire is that tries our lives, or whatever form it takes, its purpose is to test "what sort of work each one has done" (1 Cor. 3:13). Many Christians are constantly involved in a whirlwind of activity for the Lord. But perhaps what they are building is nothing more than wood, hay, and straw because their motives are unworthy or they have sought the acclaim of men rather than the praise of God. The purpose for revealing our lives before the judgment seat of Christ is so "that each one may receive what is due for what he has done in the body, whether good or evil" (2 Cor. 5:10). This evaluation by fire will discern whether the works we have done were good or bad, fruitful or unfruitful.

Surviving the Fire

When Jesus looks at our life of service and evaluates it in a split second of time, he will be assessing the character of our work. It is difficult to find words to describe just how our service will measure up to God's standard, but Paul falls back on an analogy he knew everyone could identify with. He likens our service to the construction of a building. The foundation of our building is Jesus Christ. We are just builders; it is his redemptive work at Calvary that is the foundation (1 Cor. 3:11).

We work hard for years. We conduct Bible study groups. We teach our children important lessons about God. We assist the pastor and others in our church. We try to serve the community and, by doing so, to serve the Lord. But when all comes under the blazing gaze of the Judge, what will be left? When our life of service is tested by fire, what will survive?

Paul speaks of two types of building materials—one that varies in quality but survives the fire and one that varies in quality but is burned up. He taught that the survivable category included nuggets of gold, silver bullion, and costly stones. That which is not survivable included boards of wood, chopped hay for mortar, and highly flammable roof thatch.

It is evident Paul is using these materials as analogies because, let's face it, no one would build a house out of gold. Gold is precious but not very hard, just as silver is precious but not very hard. And costly stones such as diamonds, jade, and alabaster are beautiful but unsuitable building materials. Still, each of these materials can survive the refining fire, whereas wood, hay, and straw stubble could not. Gold, silver, and costly stones all represent the profitable, rewardable service that withstand our Savior's scrutiny. The others represent those things we have done that, for various reasons, are improper and cannot be rewarded.

111

A Tragic Illustration

Some time ago I was speaking at a Bible Conference on the East Coast of the United States. The concert musician that week was Steve Green. I have always enjoyed Steve's music and his humble spirit, and this concert was no different. Steve told a story that touched my heart. Afterwards I said, "Steve, that story is tragic, but it's a perfect illustration for a book I am writing about eternal rewards. Do you mind if I tell it to my readers?" So, with Steve's permission, here it is.

On February 1, 2003, we watched in horror, glued to our television sets, as a disaster unfolded before our eyes. President George W. Bush addressed the United States and announced, "This day has brought terrible news and great sadness to our country. . . . The *Columbia* is lost; there are no survivors."

The Space Shuttle *Columbia* disintegrated over Texas during re-entry into the Earth's atmosphere shortly before concluding its twenty-eighth mission. The loss of the *Columbia* was caused by damage sustained during launch when a small piece of foam insulation broke off the main propellant tank and struck the leading edge of the left wing. Columbia was manned by seven brave astronauts including Commander Rick Husband, a U.S. Air Force colonel, and Payload Commander Mike Anderson, a U.S. Air Force lieutenant colonel. Husband and Anderson were men of faith and attended Grace Community Church in the southeastern Houston suburb of Clear Lake.

Rick Husband was a close friend of Steve Green's. Their friendship had begun years earlier when Rich and his wife Evelyn had stood in line to meet Steve after a concert in Houston. Steve sang at the Columbia launch just two weeks earlier. The spouses of the crew members each pick a song for them to wake up to one morning while they're in space. Evelyn had picked Steve Green's "God of Wonders." At the concert I attended, Steve played a tape of Rick Husband communicating with Mission Control after the song was played.

Next Steve showed a photograph of his "God of Wonders" CD that Rick actually took into space with him on that fateful mission. After the *Columbia* disaster there were more than two thousand debris fields stretching from southeast of Dallas to western Louisiana and southwestern

Arkansas. Amazingly, Steve Green's CD was among the recovered debris. When Steve showed the photo of the CD, its edges were jagged, as if someone had repeatedly cut it with a pair of scissors. It had been tested by fire, but when it was found among the debris, it was scarred but in tact. Steve was kind enough to send the before and after photos of the CD to me.

The Bottom Line

Every time I look at those frayed edges I am impressed with the tremendous heat and pressure that CD was subjected to, and yet it survived. That's what the testing at the judgment seat of Christ will be like.

Here's the issue. Each of us begins our new life in Christ with the same foundation—the Lord Jesus. Each of us is responsible to build upon that foundation. And the selection of material with which we build is our own choice. We can choose what we build, and we can choose what impact our life has on eternity. The Lord will evaluate us, the fire will test us, but no one will be able to say that we weren't given ample opportunity to earn a full reward.

No Christ-follower will lose his or her eternal life at the judgment seat of Christ. We have been given this eternal life in Christ, and it is just that—eternal. Even if some of our service does not survive the fire, our salvation will. We escape through the flames by the sovereign God out of whose hand no one will ever be able to snatch us (John 10:28–29).

So build for eternity. Be like the CD that Commander Rich Husband took into space. Live wisely now so that your life of service will survive being tested by fire and you can enjoy a full reward forever.

PART FOUR

Losing Eternal Rewards

Well-known comedian, former host of *The Tonight Show*, and fellow-Nebraskan Johnny Carson will be remembered for a lot of things, not the least of which were his "I have good news and bad news" jokes. When thinking about the subject of eternal rewards, there is a good news/bad news scenario.

The good news is that at the judgment seat of Christ, everyone will receive some reward. The bad news is that at the judgment seat of Christ, everyone will fail to gain all of the reward we could have. Facing loss is never a pleasant experience, but it is reality. Not all that we do in our lives of service to the Lord will make the cut as we face our final job review. Some things, perhaps some unexpected things, will be denied eternal reward because they will not measure up to the divine standard. And other things we didn't expect to amount to much, Jesus will judge acceptable and worthy of reward.

In the chapters that follow, we will deal with questions about the painful potential of losing reward for unacceptable service. Bite your lip if you must, but losing eternal rewards is as real as receiving them.

16

IS IT POSSIBLE
TO LOSE REWARDS?

*"He has given every Christian a job. Those ignoring His
orders will feel awful when He appears."* —C. S. Lovett

AT THE JUDGMENT SEAT of Christ there will be ecstatic joy.
We will see loved ones in the Lord whom we haven't seen in years. We
will see our spiritual offspring. Most importantly, we will be with Jesus
Christ forever.

But joy will not be the only emotion we feel. We will undoubtedly shed
some tears that are not tears of joy. God has promised us that ultimately
he will wipe away every tear from our eyes (Rev. 21:4), but there would be
no tears if the purpose of the heavenly *bēma* was only to receive reward.
Two possibilities arise from the fiery trial: "If the work that anyone has
built on the foundation survives, he will receive a reward. If anyone's
work is burned up, he will suffer loss, though he himself will be saved,
but only as through fire" (1 Cor. 3:14–15).

If each of our works for the Lord withstands the trial by fire, we will
have nothing but rewards to look forward to. But it's not likely that 100
percent of what we have done has been done in a rewardable way. The

more likely possibility is that we will be rewarded for some things, but we will not be rewarded for all. There will be some things done in our lives that will be judged unacceptable. What will become of these?

According to 1 Corinthians 3:15, "If anyone's work is burned up, he will suffer loss." God cannot reward us for those works that prove to be unworthy or unacceptable. That would be contrary to his character (Gen. 18:25; Rom. 2:1–6). God must deal justly at the judgment seat of Christ. Justice demands that we suffer loss for those labors that are but wood, hay, and stubble.

Abiding and Rewards

The apostle John also implies that some of our works will be judged unworthy. The beloved disciple warned his "little children" in the faith about the pitfalls of saying they labored in love if they really lived in hatred (1 John 2:8–11). He admonished them to live a life of love and purity. But John also instructed these believers to "abide in him" (Jesus Christ): "And now, little children, abide in him, so that when he appears we may have confidence and not shrink from him in shame at his coming" (1 John 2:28).

"Abide" is a synonym for fellowship, which is the subject of John's letter (1 John 1:3–7). It means to remain in Christ or live in him in such a way that you draw on his life as the source of your own. It means you are totally dependent on him for your salvation and your spiritual strength. This is the basis of rewards or the cause of their loss—remaining in the Christ-dependent life. John is concerned that his friends live in the Lord and labor for him.

John continues by giving his reasons for urging us to abide in the Lord. He says "that when he appears we may have confidence, and not shrink from him in shame at his coming." When Christ comes to snatch his bride away and usher us to the judgment seat, we want to appear confidently before him as our Judge. "Confidence" in the Greek means "courage or boldness to speak." John's point is that although we are not sufficient in ourselves, we can be confident of reward if we find our adequacy in our dependence on Christ.

The apostle also prays that we will "not shrink from him [Christ] in shame at his coming [presence]." In Greek the verb translated "to shrink" from him in shame is in a form that means that the shame will not be a continuous state; it's a one-time feeling, and then it is forever cared for.

Loss and Remorse

So how does this work? How could you possibly feel shame at the future judgment seat of Christ? Let me assure you it's not by the Lord Jesus shaming you. This is an investigative judgment bar; it is not the purpose of the Judge to shame you. Shame comes when we realize what our own failures in living the Christian life have cost us. Our shame accompanies our loss of reward, but it will only be momentary. We do not bear shame throughout eternity. Passages like Revelation 7:17, 21:4, and Isaiah 61:7 show us that the shame of loss is short-lived.

While we all will reflect on our lives with some regret at missed opportunities or botched service, we will also realize what is ahead for us throughout eternity, and that will quickly dry our tears and be a source of endless joy. The perspective of E. Schuyler English helps: "Joy will indeed be the predominant emotion of life with the Lord; but I suspect that, when our works are made manifest at the tribunal, some grief will be mixed with the joy, and we shall know shame as we suffer loss. But we shall rejoice also as we realize that the rewards given will be another example of the grace of our Lord; for at best we are unprofitable servants"[1]

Do you remember your high school or college graduation ceremony? It is a bit like the judgment seat of Christ. At that ceremony you may have been disappointed that you didn't work better or harder to achieve better grades and maybe graduate with honors or at least with a higher class standing than you did. But the knowledge that you made it, you graduated, and you are moving on into your future overshadows any remorse you feel. At graduation ceremonies you celebrate what you did achieve, not what you failed to achieve. The same is true of the heavenly *bēma*.

In his second epistle, John expresses the same thought only in much stronger language: "Watch yourselves, so that you may not lose what we have worked for, but may win a full reward" (v. 8). The expression "watch yourselves" means "watch out" or "beware." That's how it's translated in Mark 8:15 and 12:38. John warns each of us to beware lest something nullify the works we have done. If what we've done has been made unacceptable, it will not bring a full reward. In fact, it will not bring a reward at all.

A similar idea is expressed by Jesus in the Revelation. The Lord of Glory says, "I am coming soon. Hold fast what you have, so that no one may seize your crown" (Rev. 3:11). As believers we are exhorted to hold fast those labors we have done for him. This means we should keep hold of what is ours so others will not receive it. We are not to allow our crown to be in danger of being snatched by another.

Loss by Default

But how is this possible? How can someone else receive our reward? Can they steal our crown? Not a chance. What is rightfully ours cannot be justly given to another. The only way we can lose a reward to someone else is by default, not theft.

Judas Iscariot, had he been a believer, had a wonderful opportunity to serve the Lord faithfully. But much of the work that could have been done by Judas was actually done by Matthias, the man chosen to replace him (Acts 1:26). Matthias did not steal Judas' coveted position as a disciple; he received it by default.

The Jews were God's chosen people. To them were committed the words of God (Rom. 3:2). To them was given the promise of blessing (Gen. 12:2). To them was given the knowledge of salvation (Luke 1:76–77). But Israel was a stubborn people with a heart of stone, and they rejected their Messiah, Jesus (Matt. 21:42). This opened the way for the gospel message to be given to the Gentiles. The Gentiles did not steal the gospel from the Jews. They received it by default.

Likewise, no one can steal our reward from us. That which we do for the Lord, judged pure in the refiner's fire, is ours and can never be taken from us. However, if we do not seize those opportunities, we will lose these rewards by default. Lost opportunities mean lost reward. It's no wonder that both the Lord Jesus and the apostle John advise us to watch carefully what we do and beware that no one receive by default the opportunities that could be ours, and the reward as well.

Loss by Defect

Losing rewards is possible in two ways. We may lose them by default by not seizing opportunities that are presented to us. But we also may lose rewards by defect, by living our lives in such a way that what we do does not meet the criteria to qualify for reward. This means that at the judgment seat of Christ, some of our service to the Lord could be burned because of the defective quality of the materials we used in building a life of service for the Lord. With this in mind, in the next chapter we'll look more closely at what it means to lose a reward by defective service.

17

WHAT DOES IT MEAN TO LOSE A REWARD?

"That a crown may be lost to a believer is as certain as any truth in the Holy Scripture."—D. M. Panton

SINCE THE LOSS of reward affects what we enjoy in the forever years of eternity, to lose even one little reward is a serious matter. Therefore, when the Bible speaks of losing our reward, what does it mean?

Loss Is Not Repossession

We should never conceive of the loss of rewards as a repossession. God does not take back something he has already awarded us. At the heavenly *bēma*, we do not suddenly have a quantity of rewards ripped from our hands by the righteous Judge. We are not stripped of rewards as an erring soldier is stripped of his stripes. Not at all.

The Lord grants heavenly rewards when this life is over. Remember our Lord says, "For the Son of Man is going to come with his angels in the glory of his Father, and then he will repay each person according to what he has done" (Matt. 16:27).

Since rewards are not awarded during our lifetime, the Lord could not have earlier given us a reward that would have to be returned at the judgment seat of Christ. Loss of reward is not like handing back a trophy that was mistakenly given to you. It's not returning something you earned. It's forfeiting a reward that you could have earned but failed to do so.

The judgment seat of Christ is not a time for sour grapes. We will clearly see why we have forfeited rewards, and our loss, shame, and tears will be real. That's why it's important that our Savior wipe away all our tears at the beginning of our eternity with him.

The Positive Loss

Losing a reward involves more than simply failing to gain a reward. Losing a reward is not just the absence of a reward. At the judgment seat each of our works that survive the fire will bring reward and much rejoicing. Likewise, each of our works that are burned will bring more than loss and sadness. Suddenly, a great sense of shame will come over us as we stand before our Master and realize both what we could have done for him and didn't and what we did that was unacceptable to him.

I believe the shame that will engulf us will be greater than any of us can imagine. On that day, we will have to look the Lord in the eye. We will face him and know what he knows. Maybe this is why the apostle John counsels us to "abide in him, so that when he appears we may have confidence and not shrink from him in shame at his coming" (1 John 2:28).

Perhaps the Lord will reprimand us for not laboring more faithfully. As pure service brings commendation, so impure service may bring a reprimand. Remember, in the parable of the talents, the lord commended his faithful servant by saying "well done, good and faithful servant" (Matt. 25:23). But at the same time he called the unprofitable servant a "wicked and slothful servant" (v. 26). Losing a reward is not simply the negative of gaining a reward. It carries with it all the shame and reproach due an untrue service and an unfaithful servant.

No Loss of Salvation

As we've seen, salvation is entirely different from rewards. When speaking of the loss of reward Paul says, "If anyone's work is burned up, he will suffer loss, though he himself will be saved, but only as through fire" (1 Cor. 3:15). Fortunately, when one loses his reward, he doesn't lose his eternal life (Rom. 8:35–39).

The expression "but only as through fire" simply means "as though you came through a fire." This should be of some comfort to us. Even though you or I have not been as faithful as we should have been in serving the Lord, our salvation will not be jeopardized. This will be like a man who escapes from a burning building and has to leave everything behind. Smoking embers are falling everywhere. The heat of the fire can be felt on his face. He scrambles down the staircase and darts through the door safety. He is able to grab only his laptop and a few photo albums. Everything else, all that he treasures, all his stuff, is burned up, but he himself escapes amid the flames. We may lose some rewards at the judgment seat of Christ, but we will never lose our souls. Salvation is ours for eternity.

Whether we receive a great reward or a small reward, we will still be "heirs of God and fellow heirs with Christ" (Rom. 8:17). Because of God, we have been born again "to a living hope through the resurrection of Jesus Christ from the dead, to an inheritance that is imperishable, undefiled, and unfading, kept in heaven for you" (1 Peter 1:3–4). Nothing can remove that from us.

Imagine the consternation, however, of those who, in a split second of time, will see a great portion of their life's work vanish before their eyes because their service did not pass the trial by fire. How much will this resemble Lot. When judgment came to Sodom, Lot escaped the fire but lost nearly everything he had—his home, his goods, his wife, and even his integrity and honor (Genesis 19).

That's why the apostle John makes a final appeal to all of us. He begs, "Watch yourselves, so that you may not lose what we have worked for, but may win a full reward" (2 John 8). This is a warning to Christ-followers not to become complacent about how we serve the Lord. We need to be vigilant right to the end.

Amid the shouts of joy there is bound to be some sobs of remorse and shame at the judgment seat of Christ. Each of us should be encouraged to take every opportunity to serve the Lord Jesus that comes our way, and make sure that it is done in a manner pleasing to him, the righteous Judge. "If the work that anyone has built on the foundation survives, he will receive a reward. If anyone's work is burned up, he will suffer loss, though he himself will be saved, but only as through fire" (1 Cor. 3:14–15).

18

WHAT IF I
HAVEN'T CHOSEN GOLD?

*"For my part, what I have done in the past troubles me
no more, for it is repented of and mercifully put under the
blood of Christ; but what I have not done troubles me."*
—*Leonard Ravenhill*

TAIPEI 101 in Taipei, Taiwan, is the world's tallest building. The 1,666-
foot skyscraper tops the previous record holder, the Petronas Towers in
Kuala Lumpur, by 183 feet. What made designing this 101-story building
for an earthquake- and typhoon-prone region such a challenge is that the
tower stands about 650 feet from a major fault line, and it faces winds of
one hundred miles per hours. The engineers who designed it, however,
give assurance that the building will be able to deal with either of these
tests.

When the apostle Paul wants to explain how our service to the Lord
survives the test by fire, it's no surprise, then, that he uses the metaphor
of a building. He says, "For no one can lay a foundation other than
that which is laid, which is Jesus Christ. Now if anyone builds on the
foundation with gold, silver, precious stones, wood, hay, straw—each

one's work will become manifest, for the Day will disclose it, because it will be revealed by fire, and the fire will test what sort of work each one has done. If the work that anyone has built on the foundation survives, he will receive a reward. If anyone's work is burned up, he will suffer loss, though he himself will be saved, but only as through fire" (1 Cor. 3:11–15).

The Foundation Matters

The most important section of a building is the foundation. It really doesn't matter how well you build or how much you spend on quality building materials if you erect a building on a faulty foundation.

Recently I again visited the Leaning Tower of Pisa. Construction on this beautiful freestanding bell tower began on August 9, 1173. But within five years the Italians knew they had a problem. The tower was leaning noticeably to the North. The lean was first discovered during construction of the third floor. During the building of the next three floors, the lean was corrected by building the floors parallel to the ground, and not level with the leaning building. During this phase, however, the tower started to lean the other way. At this point, all the adjustments in the world couldn't prevent the famous bell tower of Pisa from leaning. Why? It was built on unsuitable ground for such a heavy and tall building. It is only about six feet above sea level and built on a riverbed. The underlying ground is made up of layers of sand and clay. The Leaning Tower of Pisa is one of the best-known examples that prove the foundation matters.

The foundation matters in Christian living, too. The psalmist asked, "If the foundations are destroyed, what can the righteous do?" (Ps. 11:3). But the foundation for our lives and our service to God is Jesus Christ himself. No Christian can lay any foundation other than the one that has already been laid for us. We don't build the foundation; we construct the building on that foundation, and the quality of our building depends solely on the quality of material we use in construction, not on the foundation.

Our foundation isn't faulty, but the construction we do on that foundation may be.

The Materials Matter

In the metaphor of our life as a building, the materials matter just as the foundation does. One day our building will be burned, and only the appropriate building materials will survive the fire. All others will be consumed and lost forever. In view of the fact that the material we use in building our lives of service to God will be tested by fire, the apostle Paul urges us to construct our lives of gold, silver, and precious stones, which won't burn, in contrast to wood, hay, and straw, which are easily ignited and burned up by fire (1 Cor. 3:12–13).

While some writers have offered fanciful interpretations of the meaning of gold, silver, and precious stones, Scripture itself assigns no meaning. I believe they are used simply as examples of valuable building materials, just as wood, hay, and straw are used as examples of less valuable building materials. We don't need to speculate on why Paul chose these materials; we do have to make certain our lives match the right materials.

Gold has been a highly sought-after precious metal throughout history. It has been used for millennia as money, in jewelry, and it now forms the basis for a monetary standard used by the International Monetary Fund. While never deemed as precious as gold, silver also has been known since antiquity as a soft white lustrous precious metal. It, too, has been used in currency, ornaments, and jewelry, as well as utensils (hence the term silverware). A precious stone is a rare stone of high value. Gemologists usually divide stones into two categories, precious and semi-precious. Examples of precious stones are diamonds, emeralds, rubies, and sapphires. Semi-precious stones are opals, lapis-lazuli, turquoise, and topaz. The breastplate of the high priest in the Old Testament contained twelve precious and semi-precious stones, one each for the twelve tribes of Israel.[1]

On the other end of the building materials spectrum are wood, hay, and straw. While we often use wood in the construction of our homes, we know the tragedy of house fires that are fueled because of the common use of wood in floors, walls, ceilings, etc. Even more combustible are hay and straw. Buildings constructed from such materials aren't very good—just ask the three little pigs. Buildings made of gold, silver, and precious stones are far better.

The Choice Matters

The selection of building materials for our life of service to God is a personal choice. We each decide what kind of service we will have by the kinds of materials we choose. I can choose to serve in the spotlight so everyone sees me and praises what I do. I can choose popularity, pleasure, and wealth. I can choose to get by with as little service to God as possible. When I come to a fork in the road, I can choose the easy path, the well-paved road, and the one with fewer obstacles. I can opt for style over substance, less over more, ease over difficulty. But in doing so, I may well be choosing straw over silver, and that's a choice I will regret significantly at the judgment seat. The choice matters.

That's why Paul is so eager to remind us: "Each one's work will become manifest, for the Day will disclose it, because it will be revealed by fire, and the fire will test what sort of work each one has done. If the work that anyone has built on the foundation survives, he will receive a reward. If anyone's work is burned up, he will suffer loss . . ." (1 Cor. 3:13–15).

If all that you and I enjoy for eternity is determined at the judgment seat of Christ, and if the quality of the work (building materials) will be tested by fire on that day and the true character will be revealed, what must we do to insure that we will not suffer a horrible loss in the fire? We have to become aware of what Jesus our Judge is looking for in our lives. We need to gain some biblical insight into what constitutes acceptable service and what is just a bubble floating toward a waiting pin. In short, we need to steel our minds with what the Bible says about the judgment seat of Christ so we minimize the sorrow and loss we could experience on that day. We need to know what criteria Jesus will use to judge our lives acceptable.

PART FIVE
The Criteria Used to Judge Us

As a student for many years and later as a college and university professor, I noticed a lot of interest in a system of justice known as "grading on the curve." The curve system allows the student's grade to fluctuate according to the scholastic ability of the class. What might earn a student a C in one class could be an A in a class with less gifted students.

God, however, does not grade on the curve. With respect to salvation, God does not say, "I know you're all failures, but I'll take the top third of you failures into heaven." God grades against a standard of excellence. He explicitly says, "For all have sinned and fall short of the glory of God" (Rom. 3:23). God's criterion is Christ. When we are compared with the perfect life of God the Son, we just don't measure up. God doesn't overlook that; he does something about it. He makes us measure up by imputing to us the righteousness of Jesus Christ (2 Cor. 5:21). We who have fallen short of the minimum requirement for acceptance into heaven have been made fit for entrance by receiving Jesus Christ as Savior.

Just as God has a criterion for accepting us in salvation, he has certain criteria for judging our service to be acceptable. As has already been noted, not all that we do in Jesus' name will be accepted by him as legitimate service. Only that which proves authentic through the fiery test will last. Only what our Judge discerns as measuring up to the criteria will be acceptable. So what are the criteria by which our life of service will be judged? What is Christ the Judge looking for? Answers may vary widely, but let me suggest the most obvious.

19

DO MY SOURCES MATTER?

"I value all things only by the price they shall gain in eternity."—John Wesley

DO YOU REMEMBER Jayson Blair? People in the cubicles at the *New York Times* do. On April 28, 2003, the *Times* national editor, Jim Roberts, questioned Blair about similarities between a story he had written two days earlier and one written by San Antonio *Express-News* reporter Macarena Hernandez on April 18. Hernandez contacted the *Times* after details and quotes in Blair's story appeared exactly the same as hers.

Blair had plagiarized the San Antonio reporter's article. The *Times* editors commissioned an internal report from a committee of twenty-five staffers and three outside journalists. The investigators discovered that thirty-six of the seventy-three national news stories Blair had written since October 2002 were suspect, ranging from fabrications to copying stories from other sources. It was a significant embarrassment to the *New York Times* and a smudge on the integrity of one of the nation's leading newspapers.

Jayson Blair got himself into trouble because he was not honest about his sources. His sources were not inaccurate, but he ascribed work to himself rather than to another reporter.

God is very interested in our sources. He wants us to use the power of an appropriate source when we serve him and to recognize that we are not that source. Like Jayson Blair, we can ascribe our work to the rightful source, or we can claim to be that source ourselves. If we claim to be our own source, we are headed for devastating disappointment at the heavenly *bēma*.

The Christ-in-You Principle

Of all the criteria the Lord Jesus will use at the judgment seat of Christ to discern the acceptability of our service, the first is what we might call the Christ-in-you principle of Galatians 2:20. It gets to the heart of who actually did the work you are presenting at the *bēma*, Christ or you.

Paul declares in Galatians 2:20, "I have been crucified with Christ. It is no longer I who live, but Christ who lives in me. And the life I now live in the flesh I live by faith in the Son of God, who loved me and gave himself for me." Two key clauses in this verse produce the Christ-in-you principle: "I have been crucified with Christ" and "Christ lives in me."

The order in which the words appear in the first clause is significant. The text actually says "with Christ I have been crucified." This order, with Christ being first, puts the emphasis on the crucified One and not on the process of our crucifixion with him. Many get this turned around. They talk all the time about dying to sin, which sounds very spiritual, but attribute little of their power to the Christ who died for their sins.

Our Lord's death and resurrection are inseparable. The major tenet of the "Christ-in-you principle" is our special union with Christ and the fact that he is the resurrected Lord of our lives. Our service is only acceptable to God if this union exists.

The second key clause is "Christ lives in me." Paul's fellowship with the Lord began with the crucifixion of his own will on the Damascus road and his conversion from sin and death. But that fellowship would soon have dwindled if there had not been more to it than the Damascus road experience.

The basis for your conversion is the substitutionary death of Jesus Christ, atoning for your sins. But, the basis for your Christian life is "Christ in you, the hope of glory" (Col. 1:27). What makes living the Christian life at all possible is the knowledge that "Christ lives in me." He, and he alone, is the source of acceptable service.

The Battle Rages

We should remember that Christ not only gives us life, but Christ *is* our life (Col. 3:4). When we are reconciled to God by Christ's death, we find our lives so intertwined with his that we strive not to continually engage in the deeds of the flesh. However, since we are yet sinners and prone to sin, there is a constant battle raging inside us. Our flesh prods us to do those things that embarrass the Spirit who resides within us. Our new Christ-like nature moves us to live in righteousness, but since we still live in the flesh, we are prone to do those things that satisfy the flesh. Paul describes the battle in Romans 7.

In his struggles with himself, Paul learned that although Christ lived in him, on occasion he didn't act like it. This is our experience today. Christ lives in us through the presence of his Spirit, but sometimes we do things, say things, or think things that do not glorify our Savior. The happy, rewarding, successful Christian life is one in which our lives are so wrapped up in his that we constantly push our flesh into the background and engage in "Christ-in-you" activity instead.

When our life is tried by fire at the judgment seat, all that we have done for the Lord will be scrutinized by his holiness and righteous presence. Jesus Christ will approve only those of our works that meet the criteria that he has set. One of his initial concerns will be who did the work. Did we do the work in our own strength or in his strength? As a pastor, did you rely on your innate talent, your charm, or your personal speaking ability to carry you Sunday after Sunday, or did you fall on your knees each Sunday morning and ask the Spirit of God to fill you with his power? As a servant of the Lord did you just "tough it out" and hope for the best results, or did you ask God for strength that was not your own? Here's the question: did *you* do the work or did God do the work *through* you?

The Hunt for Acceptable Service

Many Scriptures indicate the Judge will approve only that which is done by his power. He will judge as worthy of reward only that which he was allowed to do through us. Anything we were able to accomplish on our own will be burned up in the fire. Consider these Scriptures:

- **John 15:5**: "I am the vine; you are the branches. Whoever abides in me and I in him, he it is that bears much fruit, for apart from me you can do nothing."
- **1 Corinthians 15:10**: "But by the grace of God I am what I am, and his grace toward me was not in vain. On the contrary, I worked harder than any of them, though it was not I, but the grace of God that is with me."
- **Ephesians 6:5–8**: "Slaves, obey your earthly masters . . . as you would Christ, not by the way of eye-service, as people-pleasers, but as servants of Christ, doing the will of God from the heart, rendering service with a good will as to the Lord and not to man, knowing that whatever good anyone does, this he will receive back from the Lord. . . ."
- **Philippians 1:9–11**: "And it is my prayer that your love may abound more and more, with knowledge and all discernment, so that you may approve what is excellent, and so be pure and blameless for the day of Christ, filled with the fruit of righteousness that comes through Jesus Christ, to the glory and praise of God."
- **Philippians 4:13**: "I can do all things through him who strengthens me."
- **Hebrews 13:20–21**: "Now may the God of peace . . . equip you with everything good that you may do his will, working in us that which is pleasing in his sight, through Jesus Christ, to whom be glory forever and ever. Amen."

These verses all teach the same thing. In our lives, that which is acceptable to God is done by Jesus Christ, not by us. In our lives, that which is acceptable to God brings glory to the Father through Jesus

Christ, not glory to us. Any service we have rendered for the sake of the gospel that has been done independently of him will not bring ultimate glory to God, nor will it bring reward to us. Much of what we do, even in the Lord's name, may appear in the eyes of men as great service to God, but if it was done on our own power, apart from his indwelling strength, it will be of no value. It will not be able to withstand being tested by fire.

Jesus Christ is looking for people who will be vessels. He wants to fill us with himself; he doesn't want us to be full of ourselves. He wants to win the lost through us; he doesn't want us to try and win the lost. He is the worker; we are the vessels. The work is his when we are his. The work is ours when we are ours. We must live in the Spirit of God, but more importantly, he must live in and work through us.

When our labors for the Lord are judged at the heavenly *bēma*, they will be judged according to whether we have done them or Christ has done them. A major criterion for reward is the source of strength through which our life of service has been lived. Things done in the flesh will result only in the disappointment of rejection. Things done in the Spirit will result in the delight of reward. The glory will be Christ's, but the reward will be ours. Without the Christ-in-you principle, there is no reward. God is interested in the source of your life of service because only when he is the source is your service rewardable.

20

DOES MY FAITHFULNESS COUNT?

"[The Judgment seat] is meant for us professing Christians, real and imperfect Christians; and it tells us that there are degrees in that future blessedness proportioned to present faithfulness."—Alexander Maclaren

WEBSTER DEFINES FAITHFULNESS as loyalty, reliability, or dependability, marked by a strong sense of duty or responsibility. But faithfulness is not always evident in our society today. Look around you. Examples abound.

Profiles International, a human resources specialist, estimates that in a company of one hundred employees, typical absenteeism costs that company about $1,899 per day.[1] Today's families are being torn apart by a lack of faithfulness. The divorce rate in the United States hovers around 0.38 percent divorces per capita per year.[2] And now there is another threat to faithfulness in marriage—virtual unfaithfulness. Pornography allows people to be mentally unfaithful to their spouse; the availability of pornography, thanks to the Internet, is prolific. "We live in a

Pornotopia," says J. Budziszewski, associate professor in the Government and Philosophy departments of the University of Texas at Austin.[3]

The Christian religion places great importance on the faithfulness of the follower of Christ. We can't excuse our infidelity to the Lord because "everybody's doing it" or because we don't see faithfulness in abundance around us today. We are called to be different. Unlike those who stumble at every opportunity for sin, the apostle Peter says, "But you are a chosen race, a royal priesthood, a holy nation, a people for his own possession, that you may proclaim the excellencies of him who called you out of darkness into his marvelous light" (1 Peter 2:9). For the believer, faithfulness counts.

Faithfulness Means Trustworthiness

In the Bible, God values faithfulness. He equates faithfulness with trustworthiness. God views faithfulness as a character trait that belongs to quality people or things. In fact, the Bible reserves the word "faithful" for three things: (1) God himself; (2) God's Word; and (3) God's people who are faithful to God and his Word.

God often asserts his own faithfulness as evidence of his character. God's faithfulness is never-ending (Deut. 7:9; Pss. 89:1; 119:89–94). It is a renewable resource (Lam. 3:22–26), reflected in all he does. God's faithfulness keeps us from evil (2 Thess. 3:3; 1 Cor. 10:13) and helps us up when we fall (1 John 1:9). God's faithfulness is evident even when bad things happen to us (Ps. 119:71, 75, 81–82, 88). He is faithful in all he does because God is faithful in all he is (1 Thess. 5:24; 2 Tim. 2:7–13; Heb. 10:23).

God's Word reflects the same character as its author. The psalmist knew this when he said, "All Your commandments are faithful . . . . Forever, O LORD, Your word is settled in heaven" (Ps. 119:86, 89, NKJV). He said again in verses 137–138, "Righteous are you, O LORD, and right are your rules. You have appointed your testimonies in righteousness and in all faithfulness." The prophets knew what the psalmists knew: God's Word is trustworthy. "O LORD, you are my God; I will exalt you; I will praise your name, for you have done wonderful things, plans formed of old, faithful and sure" (Isa. 25:1). Notice the link between God and his faithful plans, which are revealed in his faithful Word. The apostles knew this, too. Paul said of an elder, "He must hold firm to the trustworthy word as taught, so that he may be able to give instruction in sound doctrine and also to rebuke those who contradict it" (Titus 1:9). Again, notice the link between the trustworthiness of God's Word and the trustworthiness of those who give instruction from it.

God's servants are also sometimes called faithful in the Bible—servants who do not cheat their master or usurp their master's position. The Bible describes many faithful servants: Moses (Num. 12:7–8; Heb. 3:2), Abraham (Gal. 3:9), Daniel (Dan. 6:4), Paul (1 Tim. 1:12), Tychicus (Eph. 6:21), Epaphras (Col. 1:7), Onesimus (Col. 4:9), Silvanus (1 Peter 5:12), and others. After the wall of Jerusalem was rebuilt by Nehemiah and his dedicated workmen, Nehemiah wanted to reward his brother, Hanani, by giving him charge over Jerusalem, "for he was a more faithful and God-fearing man than many" (Neh. 7:2).

John tells us in Revelation 17:14 that those who accompany the Lamb into battle and are victorious are "called and chosen and faithful." The Lord commended a certain Antipas and the church in Pergamum: "I know where you dwell, where Satan's throne is. Yet you hold fast my name, and you did not deny my faith even in the days of Antipas my faithful witness, who was killed among you, where Satan dwells" (Rev. 2:13).

Paul counseled young Timothy to commit the precious truths that he had heard from him and other witnesses "to faithful men who will be able to teach others also" (2 Tim. 2:2). The Scriptures place a premium on faithfulness, and nowhere will that character quality be more important than at the judgment seat of Christ.

A Faithful Steward

Paul reminds the Corinthians that he must give an account of himself as a minister of Christ and a steward of the mysteries of God (1 Cor. 4:1). A steward is a manager or superintendent of another's household or property. He is not a butler or a custodian, but more of a guardian or overseer. This was a very respectable occupation in Bible times, as witnessed by the prominent people who had stewards; for example, Abraham (Gen. 15:2); Joseph (Gen. 43:19); King David (1 Chron.

27:25–31); Israel's King Elah (1 Kings 16:9); and King Herod Antipas (Luke 8:3).

As the parable of the talents (Matthew 25) indicates, a good steward not only oversees that which is entrusted to him, but also uses it, invests it, and makes it produce for his master.

As a steward of the mysteries of God, those divine truths known only by revelation, Paul knows that he must put to work what he has experienced in Christ and produce fruit from it. So he warns, "Moreover, it is required of stewards that they be found trustworthy" (1 Cor. 4:2). Paul's desire was to be found a faithful steward in the sight of his fellow believers and especially in the sight of God.

This is the command of John to Gaius: "Beloved, it is a faithful thing you do in all your efforts for these brothers, strangers as they are" (3 John 5). As stewards of the knowledge of salvation and as servants of the Most High God, we must be faithful to our service for the Lord. "Be faithful unto death, and I will give you the crown of life," says the Master (Rev. 2:10). The Lord expects us to be faithful. He judges us accordingly.

When I came into the family of God, God entrusted to me a sovereign deposit (like the talent in the parable) and said, in effect, "Now take it and trade with it. Use it. Show me what kind of commitment you have to advancing my kingdom. If you do nothing with it, you will get nothing from it." That's also the meaning of 1 Corinthians 3:12–15.

We are to be found faithful whether our service for the Lord is large or small. Jesus gave us a principle when he said, "One who is faithful in a very little is also faithful in much, and one who is dishonest in a very little is also dishonest in much" (Luke 16:10). If we love the Lord as we should, we will then be faithful in a small, unnoticed task just as we would in a large, spotlighted task. Our faithfulness doesn't stem from the nature of the task but from our love for the Master. If the Lord truly has control of our lives, we will be faithful in any task, large or small.

Increased Stewardship

Yet there is something more. In the parable of the talents the master said to the servant who received five talents and doubled them, "Well done, good and faithful servant. You have been faithful over a little; I will set you over much. Enter into the joy of your master" (Matt. 25:21). When we are found faithful in performing a small service for the Lord, he will entrust us with a greater service, which, in turn, will bring a greater reward.

Luke records Jesus' parable of the unjust steward in which Jesus cautions the steward, "If then you have not been faithful in the unrighteous wealth [money], who will entrust to you the true riches? And if you have not been faithful in that which is another's, who will give you that which is your own?" (Luke 16:11–12). Responsibility breeds responsibility; if the servant is unfaithful, he may not be given additional opportunity for service.

This should be a great incentive for each of us to be faithful in whatever the Lord has given us to do as servants and stewards. Whether it brings a reward or not, "it is *required* of stewards that they be found trustworthy" (1 Cor. 4:2). But faithfulness is one of the criteria Jesus will use in judging rewardable service. God is interested in your faithfulness, and you should be, too.

21

WHAT IF I HAVE LIMITED OPPORTUNITY OR ABILITY?

"With many disciples the eyes are yet blinded to this mystery of rewards, which is an open mystery of the Word. It must be an imputed righteousness whereby we enter; but having thus entered by faith, our works determine our relative rank, place, reward."—A. T. Pierson

THE THOUGHT OF FAITHFULNESS and greater responsibility naturally prompts a question about another criterion used by Jesus at the heavenly *bēma*—the criterion of proportion.

"Some of us," muses Erwin Lutzer, "have had more widespread influence than others. Many who have served in mission fields can claim but few converts after lives of hardship and intense personal cost. Others are called to vocations in factories, farms, and within the home; some serve for many years, others for a few. We will not be rewarded by a scale that asks for the number of souls saved, the number of sermons preached, or the number of books written. Comparisons with someone else will be off-limits."[1]

Perhaps the most encouraging of the criteria used by Jesus at the judgment seat is proportion. By proportion I mean that Jesus will judge your work for him in relation to your ability to work. If you are simply unable to sing a song for his glory, the Lord will not condemn you for declining to sing in the church choir. And he won't condemn the choir director for not asking you. If you weren't genuinely called to be a preacher of the Word, the righteous Judge will not deny you a reward because you were a Christian farmer. If you have a friend of limited mental ability, your friend may love the Lord deeply but will not be denied reward at the heavenly *bēma* because he or she lacked the ability to serve the Lord in a capacity greater than they did. "Far be that from you! Shall not the Judge of all the earth do what is just?" (Gen. 18:25). The righteous Judge does not deny us rewards because we lack opportunity or ability. He judges us only in proportion to our abilities and the opportunities he has given us.

Proportion of Ability

We are told at the beginning of the parable of the talents in Matthew 25 that the lord of the servants "gave . . . to each according to his ability" (Matt. 25:15). It wasn't the man with the greatest ability who received only one talent, but the man with little ability. He who had the least ability also had the least responsibility. The same is true with our Lord. He does not ask us to do more than he will enable us to do. He does not ask, however, any less.

Notice, too, the lord rewarded his servants in proportion to what they had accomplished. The man who received five talents worked faithfully and produced five more talents, doubling his original holding. His lord was pleased (Matt. 25:21). The man to whom the lord gave only two talents worked just as faithfully and doubled his talents. The lord was also pleased (Matt. 25:23).

Was the master any less pleased with this man than with the first? Not at all. His response to both was identical (Matt. 25:21, 23). He did not chastise the second man because he had only four talents to the first servant's ten. No, this wise lord looked at the proportion of their service. He judged them according to their ability to produce for him.

It is said that George Washington Carver once asked the Lord to tell him all there was to know about the universe. According to Dr. Carver, the Lord said, "George, the universe is just too big for you to understand. Suppose you let me take care of that." Humbled, George Carver replied, "Lord, how about a peanut?" The Lord said, "Now, George, that's something your own size. Go to work on it and I'll help you."[2]

From the simple peanut Dr. Carver developed three hundred derivative products—among them cheese, milk, coffee, flour, ink, dyes, plastics, wood stains, soap, linoleum, medicinal oils, and cosmetics. He made a great contribution to society, but did so in proportion to his human ability to understand what God had placed before him. Performance is judged according to proportion of ability and opportunity.

Jesus is not so much interested in the talent or ability we have as he is with what we do with that ability. It has been said that he does not look at the check but at the balance on the stub. The Lord is concerned with what proportion of our ability to serve him we actually use. He will reward us in that proportion. It was only the unprofitable servant of Matthew 25 who displeased his lord because he put no portion of his talent to work.

In the parallel parable of Luke 12, an additional element is added to proportion as a criterion for our reward. Here Jesus relays a story about a manager who was set over his master's household. That manager would not slough off his duties until the day before his master returned because that could be on the day he least expected. From this the Savior taught that God is interested in those servants who are faithful day in and day out right to the end and adds, "Everyone to whom much was given, of him much will be required" (Luke 12:48). What a frightful thought for any unfaithful Christian!

We should be thankful for all the talent, abilities, and knowledge that the Lord has given us. However, Luke's account clearly indicates that we will be required to produce for the Lord only in proportion to whatever talent, ability, and knowledge he has given us. Responsibility walks hand in hand with ability and opportunity. Are you using all the talents the Lord gave you? Paul cautioned Timothy, "Do not neglect the gift you have, which was given you . . ." (1 Tim. 4:14). Using the ability the Lord

THE CRITERIA USED TO JUDGE US

has given us for his service will make that ability shine like a much-used plow. Neglecting it will allow it to rust.

On that great day when all of our earthly labors for the Lord will be judged, Jesus Christ will deal with us in utter fairness. No one will be able to say, "You judged me too harshly," for we will be judged in proportion to our capacity to serve him. May we always serve him to full capacity.

Proportion of Opportunity

"But what about me?" you ask. "I didn't become a Christian until later in life. Am I to be penalized throughout eternity because I did not have the years of service my neighbor had who was saved in his teens?" No, you are not!

Again proportion is the key. Not only are we judged according to the proportion of our ability to serve the Lord, but we are also judged according to the proportion of our opportunity.

Rewards are gained through service. Service can be done only by a servant; that is, one whose Master is Jesus Christ. You can't be a servant until you first receive the Master as Savior and Lord. Service begins when the Lord begins to take account of your ability and opportunity to serve him. If you have only been saved for three years, you will not be cheated because someone else had thirty years of service. Your reward will be in proportion to the opportunity you have had to be a loyal servant.

It appears from the teaching of Matthew 20:1–16 that a believer who lives for but a few years is able to earn as much reward as the one who lives for many years. Each of the workers, although they became laborers at different times during the day, received no less than they were promised. Each steward will receive no less than he has been promised by the Reward Giver, whether he lives a short time or a long time.

Proportion, as a criterion for our judgment, assures you that you are at no handicap if you but "fear the Lord and serve him faithfully with all your heart. For consider what great things he has done for you" (1 Sam. 12:24).

So, take every opportunity you have. Use every ability God has given you. Don't worry about others. If you do all that God enables you to do, the judgment seat will be a welcome experience.

22

HOW IMPORTANT ARE MY MOTIVES?

"If we would have people who have come to faith in Jesus Christ focus more on the judgment seat of Christ . . . they would agree with Paul that these light momentary afflictions are producing for them an eternal and exceedingly heavy weight of glory." —Earl Radmacher

MOTIVATION PLAYS a critical role in what is judged acceptable at the judgment seat of Christ. It is fine to be faithful in laboring for the Lord, indeed it is required, but it is also necessary that faithfulness arise out of pure motivation.

We have all been exposed to motivational speakers and books on motivation and motivational theory. There is a huge discussion in psychology circles today about the root causes of motivation. When Abraham Maslow introduced his five-tiered "hierarchy of needs" in 1943, the discussion had seemed to come to an end. But many have challenged the ability to rank our personal needs, and Maslow knew nothing of Spirit-controlled motivation. Most motivational theory among secularists tends to focus on the self; motivational theory among Christ-followers must steer away from self and focus on serving the Savior.

A Bible study group leader may be extremely faithful in the preparation and presentation of her study. She may build the biggest group in the state. But if the group leader's primary motivation is to be invited as a speaker at some national conferences, her motive cancels any possibility of receiving praise from the Lord.

A pastor and his people may work very hard visiting, ministering to, and evangelizing their community, but if their motive is to be known as the fastest growing church in the city, their faulty motives preclude the possibility of reward at the heavenly *bēma*. Jesus said, "Truly I say to you, they have received their reward" (Matt. 6:2, 5).

Using the Right Criterion

Please do not misunderstand. This is not to say the church that is the fastest growing is improperly motivated. God blesses his work, and many churches who desire to bring glory to God through the salvation of the lost have indeed become the fastest growing. There will come a day when they shall be rewarded. But the criterion used at the judgment seat of Christ is not size or fame but motivation.

Paul cautions the Corinthian believers against judging the standing of other Christians: "Therefore do not pronounce judgment before the time, before the Lord comes, who will bring to light the things now hidden in darkness and will disclose the purposes of the heart. Then each one will receive his commendation from God" (1 Cor. 4:5). There may be things praiseworthy about some believers that we have never noticed. In fact, some Christian workers we have criticized most severely could receive more praise and reward than we do.

The Lord will bring to light, as well, things that all of us would rather have remained in the darkness—things we're not very proud of. On that day there will be cause both for praise and for shame. Since we don't know the proportion of each in our fellow laborers, we are best advised not to do much finger pointing now.

Open Heart Scrutiny

Paul also warns that the Lord "will disclose the purposes of the heart" (1 Cor. 4:5). There is little doubt but that he is talking about our motives. Not only will our service be brought to light but also the reason behind that service.

In all probability there will be cases in which some service may be worthy of reward but will be nullified by the shameworthy motive that produced it. It's easy for Christians to be puffed up in pride over what they are doing for the Lord. If the Lord has blessed you with a pleasing personality, good platform ability, or unusual talent, there is a real danger that you could fall victim to self-glorification instead of directing the glory heavenward. When our labors begin to bear fruit, how much more frequently are we tempted to count hands and cards than to count God faithful. God counts hearts, not hands. He is pleased with what he can do through us, not what we can do for him.

Don't be fooled, however. God is not pleased with those who claim to be fruitful but have no fruit to attest to it. We cannot and dare not excuse our failures by saying, "Oh well, at least I'm faithful." Neither can we say, "I may not be bearing fruit but at least my motives are pure." God is looking for faithful, successful servants who have both God-honoring methods and motives.

Always on Guard

Jesus spoke of people who do good for the wrong motive. Our Lord said:

> Beware of practicing your righteousness before other people in order to be seen by them, for then you will have no reward from your Father who is in heaven.
>
> Thus, when you give to the needy, sound no trumpet before you, as the hypocrites do in the synagogues and in the streets, that they may be praised by others. Truly, I say to you, they have received their reward. But when you give to the needy, do not let your left hand know what your right hand is doing, so that your giving may be in secret. And your Father who sees in secret will reward you.

And when you pray, you must not be like the hypocrites. For they love to stand and pray in the synagogues and at the street corners, that they may be seen by others. Truly, I say to you, they have received their reward (Matt. 6:1–5).

Alms-giving and praying were two commendable practices, but the reasons they were practiced were contemptible. Good done for the wrong reason is no good at all.

God-Worthy Motivation

So what should our motivation be? Does the Bible give us any help? It does. There are many motivating factors to serving the Lord, but these "Top Ten" ought to get us started.

- **Motivation 1: The Desire to Love the Master.** Jesus said, "If you love me, you will keep my commandments" (John 14:15). Also, there is this in verse 21: "Whoever has my commandments and keeps them, he it is who loves me. And he who loves me will be loved by my Father, and I will love him and manifest myself to him." And don't forget John's words: "For this is the love of God, that we keep his commandments" (1 John 5:3).
- **Motivation 2: The Desire to Avoid God's Discipline.** This is the flip side of service out of love, but it is nonetheless a motivation for acceptable service. This is sometimes referred to as serving with "the fear of the Lord." Acts 9:31 notes, "So the church throughout all Judea and Galilee and Samaria had peace and was being built up. And walking in the fear of the Lord and in the comfort of the Holy Spirit, it multiplied." Philippians 2:12 says, "Therefore, my beloved, as you have always obeyed, so now, not only as in my presence but much more in my absence, work out your own salvation with fear and trembling."
- **Motivation 3: The Desire to Have a Clear Conscience.** Let's face it: often we are motivated to serve the Lord in order

to have a clear conscience. Paul says, "The aim of our charge is love that issues from a pure heart and a good conscience and a sincere faith" (1 Tim. 1:5). Paul himself admits to this motivation when he says, "I thank God whom I serve, as did my ancestors, with a clear conscience, as I remember you constantly in my prayers night and day" (2 Tim. 1:3). And Peter admonishes us, "always being prepared to make a defense to anyone who asks you for a reason for the hope that is in you; yet do it with gentleness and respect, having a good conscience, so that, when you are slandered, those who revile your good behavior in Christ may be put to shame" (1 Peter 3:15–16).

- **Motivation 4: The Desire for Usefulness.** The apostle's words ring with clarity: "Now in a great house there are not only vessels of gold and silver but also of wood and clay, some for honorable use, some for dishonorable. Therefore, if anyone cleanses himself from what is dishonorable, he will be a vessel for honorable use, set apart as holy, useful to the master of the house, ready for every good work" (2 Tim. 2:20–21). What's the point in being Christ's vessel if we aren't fit to be used?

- **Motivation 5: The Desire for Friends and Family to Be Saved.** A chief motivating factor for our acceptable service to the Lord, if we are properly motivated, is to see the lost be born from above, born again by God's grace into eternal salvation. Peter's words to believing wives reflect this motivation: "Likewise, wives, be subject to your own husbands, so that even if some do not obey the word, they may be won without a word by the conduct of their wives, when they see your respectful and pure conduct" (1 Peter 3:1–2). And Peter's words in 1 Peter 3:15–16 quoted above also display this motivation.

- **Motivation 6: The Desire for a Deeper Walk with God.** The apostle John warns, "If we say we have fellowship with him while we walk in darkness, we lie and do not practice the truth. . . . Beloved, if our heart does not condemn us, we have confidence before God; and whatever we ask we receive from him, because we keep his commandments and do what pleases him" (1 John 1:6; 3:21–22). This reflects the motivation of the sons of Korah when they wrote in Psalm 42:1–2, "As a deer pants for flowing streams, so pants my soul for you, O God. My soul thirsts for God, for the living God." Pleasing God and thirsting for him will bring more motivation to serving him than rewards ever will. Our service to God is out of a desire to walk so closely behind him that even our gait resembles his.

- **Motivation 7. The Desire to Do the Right Thing.** The psalmist didn't say, "I desire to do your will, O my God; your law is within my heart" for what he would get out of it. We don't do God's will merely for reward; we do it because it's right. It's God's will. Paul says, "Finally, brothers, whatever is true, whatever is honorable, whatever is just, whatever is pure, whatever is lovely, whatever is commendable, if there is any excellence, if there is anything worthy of praise, think about these things" (Phil. 4:8). God wants our minds to be focused on those things that can receive impulses about his will. We must concentrate on those things that will count for eternity and not just think about things that benefit us in time. When we desire to do the right thing, we will desire to do the rewardable thing.

- **Motivation 8. The Desire for Personal Peace.** Paul continued, "What you have learned and received and heard and seen in me—practice these things, and the God of peace will be with you" (Phil. 4:9). The writer of Hebrews seems to be alluding to the desire for peace and joy as a result of serving the Lord acceptably when he says, "Therefore, since we are surrounded by so great a cloud of witnesses, let us also lay aside every weight, and sin which clings so closely, and let us run with endurance the race that is set before us, looking to Jesus, the founder and perfecter of our faith, who for the joy that was set before him endured the cross, despising the shame, and is seated at the right hand of the throne of God" (Heb. 12:1–2).

- **Motivation 9. The Desire for Present Blessing.** Peter understood this desire when he wrote, "Do not repay evil for evil or reviling for reviling, but on the contrary, bless, for to this you were called, that you may obtain a blessing. For 'Whoever desires to love life and see good days, let him keep his tongue from evil and his lips from speaking deceit; let him turn away from evil and do good; let him seek peace and pursue it. For the eyes of the Lord are on the righteous, and his ears are open to their prayer. But the face of the Lord is against those who do evil'" (1 Peter 3:9–12). In order to obtain a blessing we must first be a blessing.

- **Motivation 10. The Desire for Eternal Reward.** Jesus said it best: "Do not lay up for yourselves treasures on earth, where moth and rust destroy and where thieves break in and steal, but lay up for yourselves treasures in heaven, where neither moth nor rust destroys and where thieves do not break in and steal. For where your treasure is, there your heart will be also" (Matt. 6:19–21). Consider also Luke 19:17–19; 1 Corinthians 3:12–15; and 2 Corinthians 5:9–10.

Each of us must constantly examine the motives for our service to the Lord. We cannot be rewarded for that which does not meet the criterion of pure motive—to glorify God. That which is self-motivated is unmerited. That which is motivated by a love for Christ (whether or not those around us deem us a success) is deserving of reward. Success has little to do with awarding praise at the judgment seat of Christ. Motive has everything to do with it. So, what motivates you to serve the Lord?

PART SIX

What Our Eternal Rewards Will Be

If you have ever been to a Nebraska/Oklahoma football game, or an Alabama/Auburn or an Ohio State/Michigan game, you know there is one thing you'll never find in the stands—a neutral person. You either cheer for one team or the other, but never both. When you leave the game, you will be either delirious or dejected, but your emotions will not be untouched. You cannot be apathetic after such an event. There is too much at stake.

The same will be true after the judgment seat of Christ. When you have seen your life of service for the Lord pass through the refining fire of judgment, you will not be able to leave that *bēma* unaffected by it. Your labors will be accepted or rejected, rewarded or unrewarded. There will be no neutral ground.

Even if you haven't thought much about your eternal rewards until now, you won't be able to put them out of your mind after the heavenly *bēma*. Let's do some thinking about them here so we're ready when the day comes up there.

The Bible hints at various types of rewards that are available to the Christ-follower. If our work abides, we shall receive a reward. The greater the number of abiding works, the greater the number and variety of rewards. Let your mind go for a while and consider what rewards await you at the judgment seat of Christ.

23

ARE ETERNAL REWARDS JUST A PAT ON THE BACK?

"Every reward suggested is a prize of a value inconceivable by us at present, and can only be appreciated at the judgment seat." —J. H. Lowe

HAVE YOU NOTICED how many expressions in English relate to the back? When you want your supervisor to let you alone, you wish he would get off your back. Maybe there are people in your office you can't trust. You don't dare turn your back because of what they may do behind your back, or even worse, they could stab you in the back. As you can see, most of our "back" expressions have a sinister feel to them. That's why I like the expression "pat on the back." It seems more positive (but not always).

Your work team is given a challenge. You slide up to the conference table, coffee mug in hand, and bat some ideas around. As usual, some have better ideas than others. Finally a plan is conceived, and each team member is given an assignment. You work hard at your assignment. Others slough off on theirs. As usual, you have to do your job and someone else's just to get the project completed. You see, however, that the team leader is watching, and you expect she will notice the extra work you are doing.

When the plan is finished and your program is launched, it's time for the boss, the supervisor, and the team leader to congratulate each of you. There are handshakes all around. High fives. Even some kudos. But that's it. No recognition for prime performers. No special thanks to you or others who made it happen. All you get is a pat on the back. You are deflated.

Is this how it is at the judgment seat of Christ? The Master tells you how much he appreciates your service to him and gives you a little pat on the back? Does this depict what's going on at the heavenly *bēma*? Hardly.

The Praise of People

Much of the apostle Paul's ministry was spent vindicating his apostleship. He was not one of the original twelve apostles (Matt. 10:1–4), nor was he chosen to replace the traitor Judas (Acts 1:15–26). As a matter of fact, Paul was called to preach the gospel not to the chosen Jews, but to the heathen, the Gentiles (Gal. 1:15–16; Acts 9:15).

There were many charlatans in the first century who came to the newly formed churches and preached false doctrines. Thus, Paul frequently invited the first-century believers to investigate his apostleship. His argument was, "Am I not free? Am I not an apostle? Have I not seen Jesus our Lord?" (1 Cor. 9:1).

To the believers in Galatia, Paul said, "For am I now seeking the approval of man, or of God? Or am I trying to please man? If I were still trying to please man, I would not be a servant of Christ. For I would have you know, brothers, that the gospel that was preached by me is not man's gospel. For I did not receive it from any man, nor was I taught it, but I received it through a revelation of Jesus Christ" (Gal. 1:10–12).

As is the case with many of God's servants, Paul was not properly appreciated during his lifetime. He did not receive the praise of men and women. But that didn't bother him. Paul knew a day was coming when all things would be made right.

The praise Paul coveted was not that of men anyway. This was the sentiment he expressed in 1 Corinthians 4:3–5: "But with me it is a very small thing that I should be judged by you or by any human court. In fact, I do not even judge myself. For I am not aware of anything against myself, but I am not thereby acquitted. It is the Lord who judges me. Therefore do not pronounce judgment before the time, before the Lord comes, who will bring to light the things now hidden in darkness and will disclose the purposes of the heart. *Then each one will receive his commendation from God.*"

The apostle Peter echoed this same thought. He, too, spoke of the trial of our faith—a trial by fire. In his first epistle to Christians scattered throughout Asia Minor, Peter comforted them in their hour of suffering by saying, "So that the tested genuineness of your faith—more precious than gold that perishes though it is tested by fire—may be found to result in praise and glory and honor at the revelation of Jesus Christ" (1 Peter 1:7).

Peter knew that the suffering we may presently receive is of little consequence compared to the praise awaiting us after our life is tested by fire. The commendation of the Lord that Paul longed for was the same "praise and glory and honor" that Peter knew would accompany the appearing of Jesus Christ.

Better Than the Praise of People

In the parable of the talents, one of the rewards given to the two faithful servants was the commendation of their master. They had served their lord equally well and had been good stewards of that which their master had entrusted to them. Thus, after their service ended, the lord said to each, "Well done, good and faithful servant. You have been faithful over a little; I will set you over much. Enter into the joy of your master" (Matt. 25:21, 23).

How much a commendation by our Lord means to us after the judgment seat will depend on how much we love and respect him. The praise of men did not mean much to Paul, for he had not served them, and they were not qualified to judge him. But the praise and commendation of the Lord meant a great deal to him. Paul's entire life as a believer was spent in service to the Master, and the Lord is the most qualified Judge in the world. To have Jesus commend him was not just a pat on the back for Paul. It was the acclamation of the only person who mattered to him.

So who matters to you? You work well for people you admire, but when you work for the One who loved you and gave himself for you, to hear him say, "Well done, good and faithful servant," is not just a gold watch and a certificate to hang on your wall. These are the most meaningful words you can hear. If they are the only eternal rewards you and I receive, it would be enough. But wait; there's more.

24

CAN PEOPLE BE A REWARD?

"The person I am becoming today is preparing me for the person I shall be for all of eternity."—Earl Radmacher

SOME OF THE SAGEST advice of all time is recorded in Galatians 6:7–9: "Do not be deceived: God is not mocked, for whatever one sows, that will he also reap. For the one who sows to his own flesh will from the flesh reap corruption, but the one who sows to the Spirit will from the Spirit reap eternal life. And let us not grow weary of doing good, for in due season we will reap, if we do not give up."

The theme of sowing and reaping is found throughout the Bible. The wise Solomon observed, "For everything there is a season, and a time for every matter under heaven: a time to be born, and a time to die; a time to plant, and a time to pluck up what is planted" (Eccles. 3:1–2). Just as there is a season of sowing, so there is always a season of reaping. The one season depends on the other.

An Unbreakable Law

Paul said, "Whoever sows sparingly will also reap sparingly, and whoever sows bountifully will also reap bountifully" (2 Cor. 9:6).

Although the apostle was speaking about giving money to the work of the Lord, this principle applies in every aspect of our lives. The more we put into something, the more we get out. The more we sow, the more we reap. The more service the Lord does through us, the more reward we receive.

As believers, we are to sow the gospel message universally (Matt. 28:19). We are to sow it unashamedly (Rom. 1:16). We are to sow it continually (1 Peter 3:15). If we do, what can the faithful servant of the Lord harvest at the judgment seat of Christ? We'll see the physical fruit of our labors. We'll meet our spiritual children as they, too, appear at the judgment seat. We'll be rewarded with seeing what God has done through those whom we were influential in leading to him. It will be the spiritual equivalent of looking at pictures of our grandchildren.

Throughout his life, Paul was concerned that he not preach in vain. He wanted to know the Lord was blessing his ministry. He pictures himself as "holding fast to the word of life, so that in the day of Christ I may be proud that I did not run in vain or labor in vain" (Phil. 2:16).

People Bring Joy

What was it that would cause Paul to rejoice? Speaking to the believers of Corinth he said, "Just as you did partially acknowledge us—that on the day of our Lord Jesus you will boast of us as we will boast of you" (2 Cor. 1:14). These carnal believers caused Paul much heartache during his life of service. Still, they will be the object of his joy. Why? Because he will meet them at the heavenly *bēma* and will be rewarded with the satisfaction of knowing that the Lord used the apostle's labor to bring them there.

Paul had similar feelings for the Thessalonian believers. Of them he asked, "For what is our hope or joy or crown of boasting before our Lord Jesus at his coming?" (1 Thess. 2:19). Paul was on a manhunt for the Lord. Through his ministry many thousands had come to know Christ as Savior, and Paul anticipated the joy that would be his when he saw them at the believer's *bēma*. The apostle wasn't bragging over the saints; he wasn't planning to parade them around the streets of heaven. He was expressing pure unalloyed joy at knowing God had used his life as a means to capture these people for eternity.

Make Some Joy

Several years ago I spoke at a Bible conference in Great Britain. Back to the Bible has had an office in the United Kingdom for more than fifty years. In fact, this conference was part of our fiftieth anniversary celebration.

We knew there would be men and women there who did not yet know the Savior, but one of the men who had received the most prayer for salvation was the husband of one of our own staff members. We'll call him Bill. Bill came along to the conference because he loved his wife, and part of her responsibilities was to staff the bookstall during the weekend retreat. The first night I preached on being below zero, not even having enough faith to believe that Jesus existed, that he died for our sins, that he was real. This is living with faith below sea level, stifled by doubt and disbelief.

At the end of the message I did not call for those who wanted to believe to come forward but simply asked them to open their eyes and raise their head, making eye contact with me. That way I would know who to pray for. Several people did, and to my surprise, Bill was one of them.

The next morning I again spoke to those who knew something was wrong in their relationship with God but couldn't bring themselves to believe what the Bible says is the cure for that broken relationship. This time, at the end of the message, I asked any who wished to talk with me to hang around after the session and I would hang around as well. Bill did not; in fact, no one did.

Later that morning, Bill came to me privately. He said, "I needed to talk with you, but after the session I had to help my wife at the bookstall." I asked Bill if he would like to take a walk on one of the trails of the retreat center. We walked and talked about the need for faith in order to be saved. The more the Spirit of God spoke to Bill through my words, the more agitated Bill became. Finally, he broke down and bawled. This giant of a man turned and gave me a big bear hug. It was evident that Bill was gloriously saved from his sin.

No one is more grateful to the Lord than Bill's wife, who had lived wholesomely before her husband and prayed for his salvation every day. The family now attends an evangelical church in Britain, and Bill continues to grow in his faith. Someday, I expect another big bear hug—again from Bill, but this time in heaven. The joy of anticipation is killing me.

What about you? Are you anticipating the smiles of joy on the faces of your spiritual children at the heavenly *bēma*? Will you enjoy a harvest of souls at the judgment seat of Christ? Remember, you only reap what you sow. To harvest then, you need to sow now. So, sow.

25

WHAT ABOUT REIGNING WITH CHRIST?

"Whatever good thing you do for Him, if done according to the Word, is laid up for you as treasure in chests and coffers, to be brought out to be rewarded before both men and angels, to your eternal comfort."—John Bunyan

ONE OF JESUS' most fascinating parables is that of the pounds or minas recorded in Luke 19:11–27. You may remember that a mina is equivalent to three months' wages for a common laborer. This parable occurs in conjunction with the conversion of Zacchaeus. The reason for sharing this parable is given in verse 11: "As they heard these things, he proceeded to tell a parable, because he was near to Jerusalem, and because they supposed that the kingdom of God was to appear immediately."

Jesus Christ was in Jericho, the city of the palms, just a short journey from the Holy City. Soon he would enter Jerusalem triumphantly, and many would proclaim him the "King who comes in the name of the Lord" (Luke 19:38). Enthusiasm was building. Excitement ran high. Many Jews thought at last they had found a political personality who would deliver them from the yoke of Roman bondage. They hoped Jesus Christ would unfurl his banner, proclaim himself king, and return the nation to the prominence of David's kingdom.

That's why the Lord spoke this parable—to paint a picture of what actually lay ahead of them—much long, hard, faithful work in his absence.

The Parable of the Minas (Pounds)

Briefly, the parable is this:

> A nobleman went into a far country to receive for himself a kingdom and then return. Calling ten of his servants, he gave them ten minas, and said to them, "Engage in business until I come." . . . When he returned, having received the kingdom, he ordered these servants to whom he had given the money to be called to him, that he might know what they had gained by doing business. The first came before him, saying, "Lord, your mina has made ten minas more." And he said to him, "Well done, good servant! Because you have been faithful in a very little, you shall have authority over ten cities." And the second came, saying, "Lord, your mina has made five minas." And he said to him, "And you are to be over five cities." Then another came, saying, "Lord, here is your mina, which I kept laid away in a handkerchief;" . . . He said to him, "I will condemn you with your own words, you wicked servant! . . . Why then did you not put my money in the bank, and at my coming I might have collected it with interest?" (Luke 19:12–13, 15–20, 22, 23).

Jesus knew that those following him from Jericho would be able to identify with this parable. During their lifetime the noble Archelaus had literally gone from Jericho to a far country. He had traveled to Rome to be awarded a kingdom from Caesar. Archelaus, too, was not well received by the citizens of Judea. They hated him and sent a hostile deputation of fifty protestors to complain to Caesar about his choice for their future king. The protest was quite successful, because Archelaus never received the coveted title of king but returned to another tetrarchy. All of these events were well-known to the Jews.

But the real meaning of the parable goes much deeper than these events. Jesus was speaking of himself as the nobleman. In correcting the flawed belief that he would immediately establish his kingdom, the Lord told those following him that he must go away, and his servants would have the responsibility of looking after his interests while he was gone.

What was he doing? Jesus Christ was foretelling that he would ascend into heaven, and those who loved him would be left behind to await his return. Like the hostile citizens in the parable, the Jewish leaders hated our Lord. They crucified him, persecuted his church, and spoke facetiously of his coming again. But, as in the parable, Jesus will come again and reward his servants (John 14:3).

What Does It Mean?

Since each servant received just one mina, it is probable that the mina or pound represents the gospel message. Each of us is entrusted with the good news that Christ came to die for sinners and is coming again to reward his saints. This mina is "the faith that was once for all delivered to the saints" (Jude 3). It is our deposit in trust, and we are to be skillful stewards in handling and dispersing it.

In the parable, the servants were told by the nobleman to "engage in business until I come." The word for "engage in business" occurs only here in the New Testament and means to "gain by trading" or "to do business with." The essential meaning of the word is seen in Ezekiel 27:9, 16, 21–22. Jesus asks us to trade in the gospel, to invest it, to make use of it. We are not by any means to hoard it or keep it to ourselves.

When the nobleman returned he immediately commanded his servants to give an account of what they had done with what was entrusted to them. The first servant said, "Lord, your mina has made ten minas more." There was no air of superiority about him; this servant was not bragging. As fiery Georgia politician Zell Miller would say, "It ain't braggin' if it's the truth." The faithful servant did not say, "I have caused this mina to become ten minas." He didn't even refer to it as "my mina." Instead, he recognized the service for which he was about to be rewarded was really not his but his lord's. He only did what was asked of him and thus rightly said, "Lord, your mina has made ten minas." He had been a wise steward.

A New Responsibility

Then something new is added. In giving a reward to this servant, the nobleman said, "Well done, good servant!" But the servant was given more than a fine commendation. He was given the authority to govern ten cities in the kingdom of the nobleman. After praising his servant, the nobleman continued, "Because you have been faithful in a very little, you shall have authority over ten cities." Apparently this was in proportion to the service he had rendered: ten pounds, ten cities.

Note that the servant whose pound gained five pounds was given authority over five cities in the nobleman's kingdom. He, too, was rewarded proportionately. Only the servant who had gained nothing received no governing authority. No service, no reward. He received in proportion to what he gave. This slothful servant even had any future opportunity for service taken away (v. 24).

What does this mean for us? Well, for those who are caught up to meet the Lord in the air, as well as those who will come to trust Christ in the tribulation (Rev. 7:14), Christ will give the privilege to reign as his fellow rulers during the millennial age. We human beings were created by God to enjoy fellowship with him and to rule over his creation (Gen. 1:26). One day we'll have opportunity to do both to the fullest, when Christ shares his regency with us, his servant-friends. Those believers who remain faithful to Christ in this age will be rewarded with a place of leadership in the age to come. This is evident from a number of Scriptures.

In Matthew 25:21, 23 (as well as in Luke 19:17, 19) the good and faithful servants were given authority over many things (in Luke, authority over cities). The faithful servant in Matthew 24:47 was set "over all his [the master's] possessions." The martyred saints who refuse to worship the beast or to receive his mark also can look forward to sharing in the reign of Christ for one thousand years (Rev. 20:4).

To the overcoming saints in Thyatira, the Lord Jesus promised, "The one who conquers and who keeps my works until the end, to him I will give authority over the nations" (Rev. 2:26). The overcomers in the church of Laodicea, those who abandon the lukewarmness that is so characteristic of that church and follow the Lord faithfully, receive this special promise from the Lord: "The one who conquers, I will grant him to sit with me on my throne, as I also conquered and sat down with my Father on his throne" (Rev. 3:21).[1]

Can this really be true? Is it possible that one of our future rewards for faithful service now is actually to share in Christ's reign on the earth? Well, what do you suppose being a fellow heir with Christ means (Rom. 8:17)? The clearest expression that one of our future rewards is that we will reign with Christ is found in 2 Timothy 2:12, which says, "If we endure, we will also reign with him. . . ." So whatever you have to endure now in being faithful as a steward of what God has given you, endure it because there's a throne in your future.

The Coming of the Great King

Jesus' parable of the minas (pounds) is a perfect picture of our relationship with Christ as servant to Master. Like the nobleman, he has gone away to receive a kingdom. He will soon return, and immediately we will give account of what we have done with what he has entrusted to us—the message of the gospel. We will be rewarded proportionately for our service to him, as were the servants in the parable.

Just as the nobleman gave his faithful servants governing authority over cities in his new kingdom so, too, Jesus Christ will award similar authority to us in his new kingdom. After the years of tribulation that follow the rapture of the church, the Lord, like the nobleman, will return. This time Jesus Christ will not appear as a babe in Bethlehem. This time he will come to establish an earthly kingdom and to institute a reign of peace on earth that will last for one thousand years (Acts 15:15–17; Rev. 20:1–6). This kingdom, prophesied in the Old Testament, will feature Jesus Christ as the absolute ruler.

This description of the kingdom closely parallels what Isaiah predicted hundreds of years before. Speaking of the Messiah, the prophet said, "For to us a child is born, to us a son is given; and the government shall be upon his shoulder, and his name shall be called Wonderful Counselor, Mighty God, Everlasting Father, Prince of Peace. Of the increase of his government and of peace there will be no end, on the throne of David and over his kingdom, to establish it and to uphold it with justice and with righteousness from this time forth and forevermore" (Isa. 9:6–7).

Although the seat of government for this political, geographical earthly kingdom will be Jerusalem (Isa. 24:23; Matt. 5:35), the King will reign over the entire world (Ps. 72:8), over all the nations of the world (Ps. 72:11). What is more exciting is that as a reward for faithful service, King Jesus has promised us a position of authority in his kingdom. It doesn't get any better than that.

If you are serving the Lord faithfully today, and your service is evaluated as worthy at the *bēma*, you will one day reign with Jesus on this earth. You may not be smoozing with high society today, but one day you'll be governing with Christ (Rev. 5:10; 2 Tim. 2:12).

An administrative position in his earthly kingdom is ours if the service we presently do is his. The more service that withstands being tested by fire at the judgment seat of Christ, the more authority will be awarded to us in the administration of the Lord's reign of peace on this earth. Being a part of that age, in our glorified bodies, is exciting enough. But the prospect of administering the universe with him should cause us to make full use of whatever gifts, skills, and opportunities he entrusts to us today. In that day, we will not be just trusted servants, but trusted rulers as well.

26

WHAT'S ALL THIS ABOUT CROWNS IN HEAVEN?

"I cannot think of a final divine reckoning which shall assign the same rank in glory, the same degree of joy to a lazy, indolent and unfruitful Christian as to an ardent, devoted, self-denying Christian." —A. J. Gordon

THE APOSTLE PAUL was fond of making comparisons between the Christian's life of service to the Lord and a runner competing in a race. He tells the Philippian Christians, "Brothers, I do not consider that I have made it my own. But one thing I do: forgetting what lies behind and straining forward to what lies ahead, I press on toward the goal for the prize of the upward call of God in Christ Jesus" (Phil. 3:13–14). Galatians 2:2; 5:7 and Philippians 2:16 reference "running" well. And the writer of Hebrews counsels us to "run with endurance the race that is set before us" (Heb. 12:1).

Ancient Gamers

Games and athletic contests were common in Palestine during Bible times.[1] And the apostle would have been even more familiar with the Isthmian Games, part of the Pan-Hellenic Games[2] held during the four-year period associated with the Olympic Games.[3] Given their frequency and proximity to ancient Corinth, it's likely he even saw an event or two. Paul knew the importance of these games and of winning. The race was the thing. The winner knew that years of training and faithfulness to his discipline had finally paid off. No winners who stood before the dais were lazy, undisciplined, or out of shape. The Greek word for "race" is the root of our word "agony." You had to endure to conquer. But having won the race, the pinnacle of human achievement was awarded to the runner—the victor's laurel.

The Olympic victor received his first awards immediately after the competition. Following the announcement of the winner's name, a judge placed a palm branch in the victor's hands while red ribbons were tied on his head and hands as a symbol of victory. The gallery of spectators would cheer wildly and throw flowers to the winner. The official award ceremony took place on the last day of the Games, at the elevated vestibule of the temple of Zeus. A herald would stand on the dais, and in his strongest, loudest voice announce the name of the Olympic winner. After this, the judge placed an olive tree wreath on the winner's head.[4]

The Christian's Counterpart

As Paul viewed these frequent athletic contests, his mind was naturally drawn to the race in which he was involved—the race of the Christian life. It's understandable that he would compare the two races and especially the laurels that awaited the victors. Hence he says, "Do you not know that in a race all the runners run, but only one receives the prize? So run that you may obtain it" (1 Cor. 9:24).

As any competitor knows, the purpose of running a race is to win. Careful guarding of our lives is necessary to make sure that we are running the best race possible. The Isthmian runners had to watch their diet, their lifestyles, and their habits. A Christian runner too "exercises self-control in all things" (v. 25). Paul further says, "I discipline my body and keep it under control" (v. 27). He did this so he would not be counted as a loser when he finished the race.

The apostle knew that by constantly taking inventory of his service for the Master and seeing if he was faithful and his motives were pure, he would not be running "aimlessly." In fact, nearing his death, he exclaimed, "For I am already being poured out as a drink offering, and the time of my departure has come. I have fought the good fight [literally, "I have struggled the good contest"], I have finished the race, I have kept the faith. Henceforth there is laid up for me the crown of righteousness, which the Lord, the righteous judge, will award to me on that Day, and not only to me but also to all who have loved his appearing" (2 Tim. 4:6–8). The apostle sounded quite confident.

Like Paul, Peter was more concerned with the heavenly crown, which will be awarded to victorious servants, than with the earthly crown that was worn by the Greek athletes. The crown we will inherit as faithful servants is described as "imperishable, undefiled, and unfading, kept in heaven for you" (1 Peter 1:4; see also 5:4).

I think it's significant that both of these biblical writers mention there is a tangible crown that awaits faithful servants of the Lord. This crown is "imperishable," that is, it will never die or shrivel up like the Greek laurel.

Two Categories of Crowns

We've already discussed the reason we receive the crown. It's a crown earned by faithful service. The very words used in Scripture for "crown" indicate that this crown is earned.

There are two words the Bible uses for crown. One is *stephanos*, a crown awarded to the conqueror or victor. It is a crown that is attained or won through achievement. In reality, it's an honorary wreath or garland (see 1 Cor. 9:25 and 2 Tim. 2:5) made of a simple branch wound into a leafy "crown." This is the familiar garland crown that adorns the heads of victors in Greek and Roman statuary.

The other word is *diadema*, a crown not awarded for achievement, but a kingly or royal crown. This crown is worn because of who you are—the king. A king wears his crown by virtue of the fact he is king. The *diadema* is mentioned only three times in the New Testament, all in Revelation. It is worn by the usurpers of the true King's authority, the red dragon (12:3) and the beast (13:1). This reveals Satan's ultimate goal of receiving the diadems that are legitimately worn only by the true Christ and King, the Lord Jesus. And, as if to stress that Jesus Christ alone is King of kings and Lord of lords, the word is also used of the many diadems the Lord will wear at his return when "the kingdom of the world has become the kingdom of our Lord and of his Christ, and he shall reign forever and ever" (Rev. 11:15).

This means that whenever a New Testament writer speaks of a crown given to a faithful servant, it is the *stephanos*, that crown that is earned. The *stephanos* is the crown of 1 Corinthians 9:25; Philippians 4:1; 1 Thessalonians 2:19; 2 Timothy 2:5; 4:8; James 1:12; 1 Peter 5:4; and Revelation 2:10. When Jesus Christ, the righteous Judge, commends us with "well done," he will also show us in a more tangible way that we have earned that "well done." He will present to us one of the crowns mentioned below.

Real Crowns

These crowns are not merely symbolic of achievement. They are not speculative. Each crown mentioned in the New Testament is found in a passage that deals with specific roles or characteristics of the Christian. They all come out of real-life situations. Since the crowns seem to be paired to various experiences of the believer, the crowns appear to be awarded as the result of being victorious through those experiences.

Some crowns are awarded for faithfulness in serving the Lord. Others come as the result of enduring a hardship or trial. Still others relate to hope and expectation. It is significant that at least five different crowns are mentioned in the Bible. Each crown is awarded for a different event, a different kind of race, a different experience in living for the Lord. Just like the champion downhill skier receives a different "crown" than the athlete who runs the one hundred meters, we, too, will receive different crowns for different accomplishments. Real-life situations result in real-life crowns.

27

WHAT IS THE CROWN OF VICTORY?

"I have held many things in my hands, and I have lost them all. But whatever I placed in God's hands, that I still possess."—Martin Luther

THE CROWN OF VICTORY is perhaps the one that relates most closely to our day-to-day living. It's given to those who know that living the Christian life is more of a marathon than a hundred-meter dash. They know the first half-dozen miles or so are relatively easy, but "heartbreak hill" is coming.

This crown speaks of toil and hardship, the ups and downs of life. It identifies the hairpin turns that can cause us to wipe out or the potholes that can cause our ride to be a little more than bumpy. But the crown of victory goes to those who are ready. They've steeled themselves in God's Word so they won't have a meltdown when things get tough.

Healthy Discipline

In 1 Corinthians, Paul was writing to a church that he had planted on his second missionary journey. Although the believers at Corinth had a good start, the sin so prevalent in their city had infiltrated the church, and growth was, to say the least, slow. Corinth was a worldly church; it failed to achieve spiritual maturity. By the time Paul wrote a letter to the church, the congregation was already split by dissention. It had deep divisions, and sin had been allowed to fester unchallenged.

In chapter nine of Paul's first letter, the apostle describes the disciplines that are part of every healthy Christian's life. These are the things believers do to grow to maturity in Christ. At the end of the chapter, Paul uses the example of an athlete who disciplines himself in order to be at the top of his game. Here's what he says in 1 Corinthians 9:24–27:

> Do you not know that in a race all the runners run, but only one receives the prize? So run so that you may obtain it. Every athlete exercises self-control in all things. They do it to receive a perishable wreath, but we an imperishable. So I do not run aimlessly; I do not box as one beating the air. But I discipline my body and keep it under control, lest after preaching to others I myself should be disqualified.

Rules of the Race

Paul had many concerns. First, when we watch a race, we anticipate who will be the first to cross the finish line—there will be only one number one. However, that doesn't mean there can't be other winners. Consider the New York Marathon. Tens of thousands run; one comes in first; thousands win. In a marathon, which is more like the Christian life than a sprint, there is more than one winner, because anyone who finishes the race is a winner. Paul wants the Corinthians to know they can all be winners, but they first have to run.

Second, the apostle believes that everyone should run to win. You don't enter the race to drop out; you enter to win. Not everyone is able to finish a marathon for a variety of reasons, but no one enters a marathon for the purpose of quitting. You run to win.

Third, everyone who runs is moderate in all things. That means a runner doesn't sit down to a Thanksgiving dinner, get up from the table, and hit the streets for the marathon. Eating a Thanksgiving dinner and running a Thanksgiving marathon within minutes of each other is not a good idea. Runners have to be temperate, restrained, and sensible. They eat in moderation as they train. If you want to win a race, you have to be sensible in how you prepare for it.

Fourth, Paul tells the Corinthians to run deliberately. This is not a practice run; this is the real thing. Christians dare not forget what their goals are if they want to win the race. You can't get sidetracked or waylaid. To achieve your goal demands a certain awareness, both of the subtleties of your enemy, Satan, and of the strengths of your Helper, the Holy Spirit. It demands a SWOT analysis (Strengths, Weaknesses, Opportunities, and Threats) of the likelihood of your success. Successful completion of your race requires the presence of mind to know how far you've come, how far you have to go, what environmental factors help you, and what factors hinder you. Simply put, it demands you be both practical and determined.

Finally, the apostle asserts the necessity of disciplined living for successful running. People don't just decide to run twenty-six miles one day. Successful marathon runners practice, practice, practice. They run. They watch their diet. They check their heart rate. They make sure they're healthy and fit. Runners are losers if they are not disciplined. It's the same for us as Christians.

In running the Christian race we have to keep an eye on our self-control, too, especially with regard to our fleshly appetites, our lusts, and our penchant to sin (Rom. 6:6). To live your life in self-control with victory over the sinful passions of your flesh is an accomplishment that cannot be achieved until you break the tape at the end of the run. It's a lifetime of starving those appetites that cause you not to be strong—appetites such as sexual immorality, impurity in your thoughts, and flashes of anger (Col. 3:5–11). In place of these you want to feast on beneficial things like compassion, kindness, meekness, and love (Col. 3:12–14). And how do you do this? Each day of your race until the final day when you finish, you "let the word of Christ dwell in you richly" (Col. 3:16).

When you run life's race as a disciplined athlete, you get the victor's crown at the goal line. It's the winner's crown, the runner's crown. And it's not a perishable crown like the Greek athletes received at the end of the Isthmian Games or the Olympics. It's an imperishable, incorruptible, eternal crown. It's the crown worn by those who have "gutted it out" and lived a life that pleased the Lord Jesus right to the final tape.

Finishing Strong

What does it look like when you've run this kind of life? It looks just like Jesus' life. It's when the Spirit of God knocks off some rough edges as you run, when you learn to run more like the Champion Jesus ran, when you're conformed to the very image of Jesus Christ (Rom. 8:29). And what's the reward for those who run such a race? It's the winner's crown, the runner's crown, the incorruptible crown. This is the crown of those who finish the race strong, though exhausted. And it's a crown you can win, if you "press on toward the goal for the prize of the upward call of God in Christ Jesus" (Phil. 3:14).

Perhaps you recognize the name Adoniram Judson? His sweet wife, Ann, and he were missionaries in India and Burma during the first half of the nineteenth century. Adoniram was arrested as an enemy agent and thrown in prison when Burma and England severed diplomatic relations. The tiny cell in which he was incarcerated was so crowded that prisoners had to take turns sleeping. There was not enough room for all of them to lie down. The combination of the hot sun beating down on them and the fact the men were never allowed to bathe made the odor almost unbearable.

One day the soldiers hoisted Judson into the air by his thumbs to torture him. Pain filled his body as he remained suspended in mid air for hours at a time. His precious Ann would come by the cell daily, look inside, weep and encourage her husband by saying, "Hang on, Adoniram. God will give us the victory." But as the days turned into weeks, Ann's visits stopped and Adoniram's loneliness increased. No one told him that his dear wife was dying. All he had was the memory of her words: "Hang on, Adoniram. God will give us the victory."

Months later, Adoniram Judson was finally released. Immediately he searched for Ann. As he approached where they had formerly lived, he saw a child so dirty he failed to recognize that it was his own. When he found Ann, she was so frail and weak from malnutrition that she appeared to be a skeleton. Her beautiful flowing hair had fallen out, and she was bald.

Adoniram called to her but she didn't respond. He took her in his arms and wept. The hot tears dropping on her face revived Ann, and she mumbled in a bare whisper, "Hang on, Adoniram. God will give us the victory."

Adoniram Judson lost his sweetheart, but not his faith and courage. He continued for forty years to minister among the people of Burma under the most difficult circumstances. When this man of God finally finished his race and was buried, scores of churches testified to the faithfulness of his labors. Adoniram and Ann Judson knew what it was to finish strong even though in the world's eyes they finished in weakness.

You and I are in that same race. We may not be miles from home, malnourished, or mistreated, but we are runners nonetheless. What will keep you from the victor's crown? Do your own SWOT analysis and determine what needs to be done for you to finish strong. "Therefore, since we are surrounded by so great a cloud of witnesses, let us also lay aside every weight, and sin which clings so closely, and let us run with endurance the race that is set before us, looking to Jesus, the founder and perfecter of our faith . . ." (Heb. 12:1–2).

28

WHAT IS THE CROWN OF BOASTING?

"Let us live, then, in the light of eternity. If we do not, we are weighting the scales against our eternal welfare."
—*Donald Gray Barnhouse*

THE CROWN OF BOASTING is awarded to those who have invested their lives in others. Often it is called "The Soul Winner's Crown" because those who receive this crown are those who have carefully, thoughtfully, and specifically invested their lives in sharing the gospel with others.

Daniel 12:3 reminds us, "Those who are wise shall shine like the brightness of the sky above; and those who turn many to righteousness, like the stars forever and ever." These are Christ's servants who have taken action and then have taken comfort in the promise of James 5:20, "Let him know that whoever brings back a sinner from his wandering will save his soul from death and will cover a multitude of sins."

The crown of boasting is for you if you are motivated by love for people and have a talent for sharing your testimony for Christ and the gospel with others. You may not have come to grips with the deep truths of the

Word, or you may never have been a leader in your church, but you have held tightly to Proverbs 11:30: "Whoever captures souls is wise."

Deliberate Lifestyle

Each of us has opportunity to bear a witness of our faith to others. There are some Christians, however, who are more purposeful in their witness. Sometimes witnessing for Jesus just happens; but it's more frequent when we deliberately seek out opportunities to tell others of him.

Abe and Marj Van der Puy served their Savior for many years as missionaries in South America. I never met two finer, more humble servants of the Lord. Marj was Marj Saint, widow of Nate Saint, the pilot who was killed, along with four others, by the Auca Indians in 1956. After Nate's death, Marj served as a nurse at the Voice of the Andes Hospital in Quito, where she brought up her three children. Abe had also been widowed when his wife Dolores died of cancer. God brought Abe and Marj together when Abe was president of HCJB World Radio, and they served the Lord together until Abe's death in 2003. I officiated at Abe's graveside service that year at a Florida cemetery.

Dr. Van der Puy served Back to the Bible as a board member for many years and was our "voice of missions" on the radio for a dozen years. When this couple came to Lincoln, Nebraska, for board meetings, they always flew on the same plane, but never in seats next to each other. In fact, they deliberately chose different seats on the plane. The reason? They wanted to create an opportunity for sharing their faith with others.

The crown of boasting is for people like the Van der Puys. If you are eager and consistent in sharing your faith with others, the crown of boasting is for you, too.

Human Crowns

Speaking of those in Thessalonica whom Paul had led to the Lord, the apostle says, "For what is our hope or joy or crown of boasting before our Lord Jesus at his coming? Is it not you? For you are our glory and joy" (1 Thess. 2:19–20). In addressing the Philippian believers, Paul also refers to them as "my brothers, whom I love and long for, my joy and crown" (Phil. 4:1).

The closing words of the book of James are powerful: "My brothers, if anyone among you wanders from the truth and someone brings him back, let him know that whoever brings back a sinner from his wandering will save his soul from death and will cover a multitude of sins" (James 5:19–20). The human soul is of immeasurable value to God. While God is sovereign even in the planning and execution of our salvation, it brings God no joy when sinners turn their back on God and refuse to come home to him. The prophet Ezekiel reminds us, "As I live, declares the Lord GOD, I have no pleasure in the death of the wicked, but that the wicked turn from his way and live . . ." (Ezek. 33:11). Jesus himself tells us, "I tell you, there is joy before the angels of God over one sinner who repents" (Luke 15:10).

It's difficult to imagine now, but there will be significant rejoicing when we see among the company of believers at the judgment seat those whom we've had a hand in bringing to salvation. "Those who sow in tears shall reap with shouts of joy! He who goes out weeping, bearing the seed for sowing, shall come home with shouts of joy, bringing his sheaves with him" (Ps. 126:5–6).

Just imagine the reunions that will take place on that day. Imagine the tears. Imagine the shouts and hugs. All because we have been faithful in sowing the seed. One of the joys of appearing before the judgment seat of Christ is seeing others there who were reaped from seed we had sown.

Just Tell Your Story

And sowing isn't as difficult as Satan would have you believe. While there are many methods for sharing your faith, the best method is your method. Just tell your story.

Remember the account of the Gadarene man who was possessed by multiple demons? When Jesus came to the eastern shore of the Sea of Galilee and cast the demons out of him and into a herd of swine, the man begged to get into the boat with Jesus and follow him as a disciple. Jesus' response was classic: "Go home to your friends and tell them how much the Lord has done for you . . ." (Mark 5:19).

Paul wasn't always successful when he shared the gospel, but that didn't stop him. He said to his Thessalonian friends, "Just as we have been approved by God to be entrusted with the gospel, so we speak, not to please man, but to please God who tests our hearts" (1 Thess. 2:4). One day at the heavenly *bēma* God will test your heart to see if you have pleased him or men. Every time you sow even the tiniest seed, it pleases God and benefits those in your life.

It's true that not all are called to preach the gospel or serve in a far corner of the world. But all of us can go home to our friends and family and simply tell them what the Lord has done in saving us. When you and I are consistent in doing that, the crown of rejoicing awaits us. This is a crown every one could receive at the judgment seat of Christ. It's a crown everyone *should* receive.

29

WHAT IS THE CROWN
OF RIGHTEOUSNESS?

"Every reward suggested is a prize of a value inconceivable by us at present and can only be appreciated at the judgment seat."—J. H. Lowe

THE CROWN OF RIGHTEOUSNESS is also known as "the watcher's crown." It's awarded to those who are longing for and anticipating the return of the Lord.

Paul had a long and fruitful life. He had much to look back on with satisfaction. Yet when he neared the end of his life, he was looking ahead, not back. He knew that because he fought a good fight, finished the course, and kept the faith, there would be laid up for him "the crown of righteousness, which the Lord, the righteous judge, will award to me on that Day . . ." (2 Tim. 4:8). Paul was confident that a crown of righteousness was awaiting him.

But the apostle adds another dimension to awaiting this crown when he says, "not only to me but also to all who have loved his appearing" (2 Tim. 4:8). When Jesus ascended to his Father, those present "were gazing into heaven." They were promised that Jesus would one day return "in the same way" (Acts 1:10–11). Believers who have become wrapped up in earthly things have their allegiance on earth. But believers who realize they are but strangers and pilgrims here and have set their affections on things above will not be contented until the Lord comes again. If you longingly anticipate that day, there is a reward for you.

Do you yearn for the Lord's appearing? Or have you become so comfortable, so invested in this world, that you no longer look for another? Do you watch for the Lord's coming, or is his return just something you talk about in your study group? There are some people who've become so wrapped up in Bible prophecy they know nothing else. These folks flock to conferences, buy CDs and DVDs of their favorite prophecy preachers, and become certified prophecy buffs. But I don't think that's what loving the appearing of the Lord is all about.

Expectations and Godliness

In the context of 2 Timothy 4, the Lord's appearing was not a platform for speculation about the end times but an incentive for righteous living. Paul fought the good fight, finished the race, and kept the faith (4:7). Based upon knowledge that he had lived righteously, he anticipated the Lord's return. And motivated by his love of the Lord's appearing, he was looking forward to being awarded a crown of *righteousness* by a *righteous* Judge. The apostle declared that all who are living righteously and who are anticipating Christ's return will share in the watcher's crown with him.

The crown of righteousness literally means "a crown for doing right." Anticipation and purity go hand-in-hand. You cannot longingly look for Christ's return and live a life that is displeasing to him at the same time. All who long for the Lord's return live like they long for it. Those who genuinely long for the "blessed hope" of the return of the Lord are the same people who live "self-controlled, upright, and godly lives in the present age" (Titus 2:12).

Note what Paul did not say. He did not say, "If you keep the faith, you will receive the crown of righteousness" or "If you are really into praise and worship you will receive the crown of righteousness." Instead, he says, "to all who have loved his appearing," this crown is for you (2 Tim. 4:8).

That's why 1 John 3:2–3 says, "Beloved, we are God's children now, and what we will be has not yet appeared; but we know that when he appears we shall be like him, because we shall see him as he is. And everyone who thus hopes in him purifies himself as he is pure."

Think about this. Adulterers, drunkards, extortioners, homosexuals, drug addicts, child abusers, wife beaters, liars, and the like are not anxiously awaiting Christ's return. If they were, they would purify themselves from their sinful habits.

Holy living is the sure sign of heavenly longing. Are those who own a Bible—the only book God ever wrote—but rarely read it ready for the judgment seat of Christ? What about those who have never considered the claims of personal holiness on their lives? Are they ready for the rapture? And what about those who have become comfortable in this life? Do you think they're genuinely longing for the soon return of the Lord and are purifying themselves as a result? Sometimes it's easy to say we are looking for our Lord's return but difficult to live in personal holiness while we wait.

Changing Our Tune

A century and a half ago the slaves of the old South had a very difficult life. They were mistreated and abused. Families were often broken up. They were treated inhumanely. And still, most of the spirituals they sang had to do with heaven and the return of the Lord. Have you ever wondered why? "Swing Low, Sweet Chariot. Comin' for to carry me home." "Nobody knows the trouble I've seen. Nobody knows but Jesus." Why were spirituals like these so important? Because for the African-American slaves, this life held no promise, no pleasure, no reward. They were looking to a distant land, a far better home. "Dis train am bound for glory, dis train."

Yet, today, the affluent evangelical rarely sings about heaven. Why? Because we have it too good down here. We're not anticipating the return of the Lord and consequently are not purifying ourselves in preparation for his return.

Stay the Course

If you're anxious to see your Savior, anxious for him to return and catch you up forever to be with him, and if you are doing your best to be spiritually ready for his appearance, you have something awaiting you at the heavenly *bēma*. It's the crown of righteousness or watcher's crown.

In writing to Timothy, Paul reminds him that there will come a time when people won't want to hear the sound teaching of God's Word (2 Tim. 4:3). Instead, they will crave sound bytes instead of sound doctrine, gummi bears instead of green beans, style instead of substance. We are already there. Yet, Paul encourages Timothy to stay the course and tells him that there will be a reward at the finish line—the crown of righteousness (2 Tim. 4:8).

The crown of righteousness is awarded to all those who practice a life of righteousness and are constantly "waiting for our blessed hope, the appearing of the glory of our great God and Savior Jesus Christ" (Titus 2:13).

30

WHAT IS THE CROWN
OF GLORY?

*"All will be in heaven, but the differences will be eternal.
We may be sure that the consequences of our character
will survive the grave and that we shall face those
consequences at the judgment seat of Christ."—Donald
Gray Barnhouse*

THE CROWN OF GLORY is a reward presented to genuine,
faithful, godly, and pure shepherds of the flock. It is the crown for service,
sometimes referred to as "the shepherd's crown."

As anyone who is a pastor will tell you, being the shepherd of a local
congregation is not an easy task. I know. I grew up in a pastor's home.
My father pastored the same church for thirty-three years. I began my
ministry as a pastor. I have an older brother who is a senior pastor. My
son is a senior pastor. And others in my family have pastoral duties as
well. I am surrounded by pastors. It's one of the most difficult jobs in
the world.

This crown is set in the context of a shepherd caring for his sheep.
Shepherds are hardworking people. I've never been a shepherd (although

I did own three sheep once as a boy), but I often have watched shepherds tending flocks large and small in the Holy Land. Their work with their flocks is more of a way of life than a job. They literally live with their flock 24/7, spending time with them and constantly caring for their needs. Sheep are not particularly brilliant animals. They tend to wander off, and they have no real sense of impending danger. Once I saw a young shepherd on one of the high cliffs above Petra carefully descending from the top to a ledge where one of his sheep had wandered. To say the least, it was a precarious climb, but sheep need a caring, consistent, compassionate shepherd, or they will often destroy themselves.

The Bible likens the pastor to a shepherd and his people to a flock. It's a tough job. Sheep wander everywhere simultaneously. It's like herding cats. Special service, however, brings about special reward. Peter indicates that the pastor will receive a reward for his endeavors in feeding the flock of God.

Not a Done Deal

The crown of glory is a reward presented to the genuine, faithful, and godly shepherds of the flock. "And when the chief Shepherd appears, you will receive the unfading crown of glory" (1 Peter 5:4). These are men who have a pure desire to see others grow in the Lord. They do this out of love for their sheep. They don't do it for denominational recognition or to write a book on how to pastor a successful church. A special crown awaits pastors for such a giving, caring life.

This crown is, of course, not automatic. When you accept the call to a local church, unpack your books, and straighten the papers on the desk in your study, you don't automatically qualify for the shepherd's crown. To be rewarded, pastors have to possess a pure desire to see others come to know the Lord and then grow them in the body. Pastors sacrifice their time, their money (Acts 20:33–35), their energy, and sometimes even their health to see those in their charge become mature saints. Pastors do this out of love and out of conviction. They do not do it for selfish motivation; if they do, they have no reward.

A special reward of glory awaits those who care for people and demonstrate it in their pastoral ministry. But not all pastors meet the exacting requirements for the shepherd's crown. Some will be disqualified.

The prophet Zechariah had stern warnings for the shepherds of God's people. He called those who had disqualified themselves by their actions "foolish shepherds" and alerted them, "Woe to my worthless shepherd, who deserts the flock! May the sword strike his arm and his right eye! Let his arm be wholly withered, his right eye utterly blinded!" (Zech. 11:17).

Problems and Possibilities

Peter notes both restrictions and cautions that apply to the pastor. "Shepherd the flock of God that is among you, exercising oversight, not under compulsion, but willingly, as God would have you; not for shameful gain, but eagerly; not domineering over those in your charge, but being examples to the flock" (1 Peter 5:2–3).

There are plenty of pastoral pitfalls listed in those two short verses. And there are other portions of God's Word that instruct us with regard to pastoral qualifications and duties. Paul enumerates these qualifications to his young friend Timothy in 1 Timothy 3:1–7:

> The saying is trustworthy: If anyone aspires to the office of overseer [pastor], he desires a noble task. Therefore an overseer must be above reproach, the husband of one wife, sober-minded, self-controlled, respectable, hospitable, able to teach, not a drunkard, not violent but gentle, not quarrelsome, not a lover of money. He must manage his own household well, with all dignity keeping his children submissive, for if someone does not know how to manage his own household, how will he care for God's church? He must not be a recent convert, or he may become puffed up with conceit and fall into the condemnation of the devil. Moreover, he must be well thought of by outsiders, so that he may not fall into disgrace, into a snare of the devil.

In that list of qualifications are many things that would disqualify some pastors today, if we took them seriously. A pastor cannot have skeletons in his closet; he must be blameless (not sinless), above reproach. A pastor must not be a womanizer. He must have his body and mind under control. He must have the gift of teaching (not just leadership skills), and he must exercise that gift regularly in order to remain a pastor.

It's evident that being the pastor is fraught with danger. One of these is at the judgment seat of Christ. Pastoring the people of God is a gargantuan task; but if faithfully undertaken, it has its rewards. Peter continues, "And when the chief Shepherd appears, you will receive the unfading crown of glory" (1 Peter 5:4). But the Bible implies that a man can be a colossal success as a pastor in everybody's eyes now and still be a colossal failure in Christ's eyes at the judgment seat.

Pastors have special responsibilities, and they have a special reward for faithfully exercising those responsibilities. The crown of glory does not imply any greater or lesser degree of glory, simply that a glorious calling, if faithfully executed, brings a glorious crown. If you're a pastor, accept the responsibility and someday the crown. If you love your pastor, pray that he will faithfully execute his responsibility so he can earn the crown.

31

WHAT IS THE CROWN OF LIFE?

"The figure of the Crucified invalidates all thought that takes success for its standard." —*Dietrich Bonhoeffer*

THE CROWN OF LIFE has also been called "the sufferer's crown" or even "the martyr's crown." It is the crown that is given to those who have suffered for their faith, even to the point of losing their life. The crown of life recognizes the value of a life well lived but torturously lived.

Has it come to your house yet? Have you seen it in your life? If not, hang on. It's on its way. What is "it"? Trouble. Trial. Testing. Tribulation.

The twenty-first century is filled with difficulty. But who am I kidding? *Every* century is filled with difficulty. This is why Jesus promised his disciples, "In the world you will have tribulation. But take heart; I have overcome the world" (John 16:33). Every life in every generation faces difficulty—sickness, poverty, pain, disease, dealing with unreasonable people, injustice—the list is endless.

But the Christian suffers from a unique form of difficulty—persecution. God has a special reward for those who endure suffering. It's the sufferer's crown, the crown of life. You don't have to go out looking for trouble to receive this crown; if you're a Christian, it will come looking for you.

No Question

Have you ever wanted to change one word in the Bible? If I could change a single word in the sacred text, it would be a word in 2 Timothy 3:12. I would change, "Indeed, all who desire to live a godly life in Christ Jesus will be persecuted" to "*may* be persecuted." There's just something so certain about the way Paul says it, as if every Christian must expect to be mistreated.

But it's true. There are many in our life, in our family, in our classroom, who despise the Lord. Because of this they will "persecute you" (Matt. 5:44). Frequently we'll endure ridicule, persecutions, afflictions, and trials for Christ's name's sake. It's not easy to bear up under these trials. No one likes to be laughed at. But we receive strength and comfort to hang in there. And the Bible says we will be rewarded for our faithfulness: "Blessed is the man who remains steadfast under trial, for when he has stood the test he will receive the crown of life, which God has promised to those who love him" (James 1:12).

Faithful unto Death

Let's face it. We live in a time when trouble is an almost constant companion. Think of the things that plague our society today. Drive-by shootings. Muslim extremists. Car jackings. Identity theft. Computer viruses. Terrorists. We now live with threats posed by what used to be just simple combinations of letters: STDs, ALS, ADHD, RLS, SIDS, HPV, and AIDS. This new century began with Y2K and has been filled with trials and troubles ever since.

Physical, financial, emotional, spiritual, and stressful challenges we face daily are pretty much a routine part of life. But persecution? Should we have to endure being persecuted for what we believe in addition to facing the glut of daily troubles everyone experiences? You might expect followers of Christ to knuckle under, give up, and be crushed under the heavy load of open persecution for their faith. But, amazingly, some believers grow in their dedication and single-minded devotion to the Lord Jesus in spite of all these things. They appear to be keenly aware that there is a coming day when Christ will reward all those who have suffered more than their share of life's troubles because they've had to endure the added stress of persecution for their beliefs.

What an encouragement and incentive this should be if you're enduring the stress of publicly announcing your belief in a Creator in a classroom where any odd belief is acceptable as long as it isn't biblical. What an encouragement if you're scorned by members of your own family, but you remain faithful as a witness for the Lord to them. God is paying attention. He sees, he understands, he cares, he remembers, he rewards.

The apostle John passes on to the saints at Smyrna what Jesus said: "Do not fear what you are about to suffer. Behold, the devil is about to throw some of you into prison, that you may be tested, and for ten days you will have tribulation. Be faithful unto death, and I will give you the crown of life" (Rev. 2:10).

Yes, trials are to be expected, if we're living for Christ. Persecutions are a natural consequence of a consistent Christian witness. But we need not fear, for the Lord will reward those who are faithful in enduring such trials and persecutions. He promises us that it will be worth it all. The crown of life is only for the saints who are willing to suffer for the cause of Christ.

It May Be Friday, but Sunday's Coming

This sufferer's crown is promised to every believer who remains faithful under trial and does not cave in when Satan's attacks are most severe. When you love the Lord in spite of your trial and are not embittered because of them, you are on your way to winning the crown of life.

Jesus' summary to his teaching of the beatitudes was this: "Blessed are you when others revile you and persecute you and utter all kinds of evil against you falsely on my account. Rejoice and be glad, for your reward is great in heaven, for so they persecuted the prophets who were before you" (Matt. 5:11–12). There is clearly a connection between bearing the cross and wearing the crown.

When he suffered and died at Calvary, Jesus demonstrated the hope that each sufferer has. For his disciples, despondent and dejected, it looked as if all they believed in, all they had worked for, all they held dear had come crashing down around them. We call the day Jesus was crucified "Good Friday," but there wasn't much good about it to our Lord's disciples. Yet Jesus reminded them that it may be Friday, but Sunday's coming. There was a reward for continuing faithfully to the end, and that reward was the bright promise of the future. More than one dear saint of God has clung to that hope in the darkest hours of life.

You don't have to read *Foxe's Book of Martyrs* to grasp what a special group it is that suffers for its faith. Just talk to a pastor in the underground church in China, a poor Christian woman who's been beaten and raped by Muslim marauders in Darfur, or an old man in prison in Indonesia for speaking out about his faith. These people are what General William Booth, founder of the Salvation Army, described as the aristocracy of heaven accompanying the King.

None of us seeks out religious persecution. Only a fool would do that. But often when and where it's least expected, being mocked, ridiculed, or even persecuted for your faith can invade your quiet life. The key is to endure it with grace and dignity, to make the Lord proud, who "for the joy that was set before him endured the cross, despising the shame, and is seated at the right hand of the throne of God" (Heb. 12:2). For all who endure to the end, God has a special reward—the crown of life. Hang in there. As Jesus demonstrated to his struggling disciples, it may be Friday, but Sunday's coming.

32

WILL I CAST MY CROWN AT JESUS' FEET?

"The deepest reward is in the very fact that we will become what our Creator intends us to become." —Iosif Ton

PERHAPS YOU'VE HEARD the Christian pop group Casting Crowns. They're a popular contemporary Christian band whose lyrics cut through the clutter and find a home in your heart. But what I like most about them is their name—Casting Crowns. What a great moniker to have for anyone who wants to serve the Lord faithfully.

Have you ever wondered about wearing those crowns we're promised in heaven? Since there are multiple crowns, and it's possible you could win more than one, how would you wear multiple crowns on your head at the same time? But will we really wear our crowns, or will we do what the Bible suggests and lay those crowns at the feet of Jesus?

Casting Crowns

Revelation 4:10–11 answers this question. Here the twenty-four elders, who are symbolic of the church, are pictured as falling down before the almighty Creator and worshipping him. As the officials of the church today, no better symbol than the elders could be used in this vision to represent the whole church (Acts 15:6; 20:17; James 5:14). Not only are the twenty-four elders engaged in worship, they are pictured as casting their crowns before the Lord's throne, saying, "Worthy are you, our Lord and God, to receive glory and honor and power, for you created all things, and by your will they existed and were created." This illustrates that the people of God recognize that their ability to serve God and every single crown that results is a token of God's grace.

As the elders worship the Creator, they cast at Jesus' feet their most prized possessions—their crowns. Think about it: casting your crown at the feet of the one who made it possible for you to be at the judgment seat of Christ. It will be a most satisfying feeling to cast your tangible reward at the feet of the King of kings.

Now you may be thinking, *But I earned it.* That's correct, you did; but don't forget that without his saving grace that provided your salvation, you would never have become a servant in the first place. No service, no stewardship; no stewardship, no crown. You would have had no capacity to earn any reward. Besides, the reward is not given for what you've done, but for what he's done through you. You were just a willing vessel. It was always his work.

Since everything of value in our lives is the result of Christ working in us, it's entirely fitting and altogether appropriate that in casting our crowns before his throne we acknowledge the Lord Jesus as the source of anything of merit in us. In the end, all the praise belongs to him for what he did through us. I don't think we will want to hold onto our crowns at the judgment seat of Christ when we realize it's by his grace that we are even there. We don't need the crowns. We need Christ.

Your Greatest Gift

What's the greatest gift you can give your Master? No question—it's your very life. Paul said, "I appeal to you therefore, brothers, by the mercies of God, to present your bodies as a living sacrifice, holy and acceptable to God, which is your spiritual worship" (Rom. 12:1). The word translated "spiritual" worship in Greek is *logikos.* It's the word from which we get our English word "logical." Your service to Christ is spiritual because it is reasonable; it is logical, because Christ died to give you life. You owe your spiritual life to him. Every Christian does. You were given life to bring glory to God.

When your earthly life is past, what better way to continue bringing glory to God than to make a secondary sacrifice by laying your crowns at his feet? The very act of placing these tangible rewards at the Lord's feet is an act of transferring the glory to the one who truly deserves it—Jesus Christ.

There is no better way to demonstrate your thankfulness to Christ than to present him with the crowns you've received. By working faithfully and thus obtaining more crowns, you will be able to honor him even more.

As those bought by the blood of the Lamb, our eternal destiny is to bring glory to him. "For you were bought with a price. So glorify God in your body" (1 Cor. 6:20). Let's do the absolute best we can for him now and anticipate the day when we can make a more tangible demonstration of our gratitude by casting our crowns at his feet.

33

WHAT WILL BE
MY GREATEST REWARD?

"Christians do not practically remember that while we are saved by grace, yet that so far as the rewards of grace are concerned, in the world to come, there is an intimate connection between the life of the Christian here and the enjoyment and the glory in the day of Christ's appearing."
—*Arthur T. Pierson*

THERE IS A FINAL REWARD that is often overlooked when people write about our eternal rewards. It's the bottom line—the most important reward we will receive.

Living a life of service for the Master is more than just a demanding responsibility; it's an exciting privilege. The sovereign God could have written the gospel message in the stars or commissioned legions of angels to share it with people. Instead, he chose inept, unworthy individuals like you and me. Unto us have been committed the words of eternal life. The gospel story, which can change the destiny of our friends and family, has been entrusted to us. It is quite an awesome thought.

When our duty as a servant has been faithfully discharged, we will stand before the judgment seat of Christ and hear our Lord say, "Well done, good and faithful servant." Feelings of satisfaction and joy will well up within us. Just hearing those words will be an awesome reward.

Likewise the Lord will entrust to us greater responsibility than we've ever known. He will award us with a position of authority in his earthly kingdom. We who today follow him will one day reign with him. Ours will be the responsibility of administering his kingdom on earth. Again, there will be a certain gratification in knowing the Lord has entrusted to us such great responsibility and privilege. This will be a very satisfying reward.

When we see those whom the Lord has saved through our labors, however, a feeling of thankfulness will overtake us, and it will be impossible to stop praising him. It will be like a grand family reunion, the likes of which we've never seen before. Seeing our spiritual offspring will be a most delightful reward.

Then the righteous Judge will award the victor's crowns. We'll feel like the ancient Greek athletes who have received the coveted laurel, only a thousand times more grateful. And when we cast our crowns at Jesus' feet to honor him, we may wonder if anything could surpass these rewards.

Above All Else

Can anything be more wonderful than receiving the Lord's commendation or reigning with him? Can there be any greater reward than seeing your spiritual children or casting your crowns? I think there can be.

When Jehovah revealed himself to Abraham as the Most High God, he spoke to the patriarch in a vision saying, "Do not be afraid, Abram. I am your shield, your exceedingly great reward" (Gen. 15:1, NKJV).

Above all else, what we shall treasure most throughout eternity, will be our intimate fellowship with the Most High God. We'll know him as it is not possible to know him now. We'll walk with him as it is not possible until all our unworthy works are burned up in the fiery trial. We'll worship him as we've never been able to do before. He indeed will be our greatest reward.

The Morning Star

When the Lord promised a position of authority in his earthly kingdom he said, "The one who conquers and who keeps my works until the end, to him I will give authority over the nations" (Rev. 2:26). Just two verses later the promise continues, "And I will give him the morning star" (2:28).

What a strange thing to say. What does the Lord mean by "the morning star"? The answer is found in Revelation 22:16: "I, Jesus, have sent my angel to testify to you about these things for the churches. I am the root and the descendant of David, the bright morning star." The Lord Jesus Christ said, "I . . . am the bright morning star." The apostle Peter also refers to Jesus in this way (2 Peter 1:19).

The greatest possible reward, the greatest treasure we will have throughout all eternity, is the presence of our eternal God. To know him and be with him forever is the ultimate reward. Who can say what internal fountains of happiness you'll be unable to suppress when he says, "Enter into the joy of your master" (Matt. 25:21).

If nothing else excites you about the eternal rewards promised to faithful servants of the Lord, this certainly must. We will be with him, enjoying his fellowship and love forever! Surely it will be worth it all when we see Christ.

Epilogue

AVOIDING HIGHWAY ROBBERY

"Consider, to provoke you to good works, that you shall have from God, when you come to glory, a reward for everything you do for him on earth." —*John Bunyan*

ALL WHO HAVE COME TO FAITH in Christ as Savior are following him on that narrow road that leads to heaven. Some are following more closely than others. It's not an easy road. "For the gate is narrow and the way is hard that leads to life, and those who find it are few" (Matt. 7:14). The simple truth is the highway to heaven is a minefield, as John Bunyan's character, Christian, discovered. Satan knows he can't change the direction of the road or keep us from our destination, but he'll do everything he can to rob us of joy on the journey and reward at the end of the road.

In this epilogue I want to share a little trick of my own about how to keep Satan from diverting you from what's really important in life. It's a simple principle, really. Start every day at the judgment seat of Christ and work backwards. Take everything you do today, every thought you think, every word you say, to the judgment seat to check out its eternal impact.

Traveling life's road with the heavenly *bēma* as a constant evaluator will help you avoid Satan's "highway robbery."

Imminent Interruption

Do you remember when you started reading this book? Did you shudder at the thought that Jesus may come again at any moment? When you realized the return of the Lord could interrupt your life's plans, how did you feel? Well, now you've come to the end, and you're closer to his return than you have ever been before. Your time to earn eternal rewards has never been shorter.

The most exciting news in this life is that Jesus Christ is coming back. What makes it even more exciting is that his return is imminent. He may come back at any time. Dr. G. Campbell Morgan, the distinguished pastor of the Westminster Chapel in London in the 1930s, used to say that he never began his work without thinking that Jesus may interrupt that work and begin his own. When you constantly live with the reality that Jesus may return at any moment, you want to make every moment you have count for eternity.

So why aren't we more intentional? Why don't we serve the Lord more diligently? Why do we spend so much time doing so many things with so little meaning? There are many reasons, of course, but I think the real culprit is none other than the old serpent, the devil. We dare not use this as an excuse, but he is a master of deceit. He knows nothing can prohibit you from entering heaven. If you're a follower of Christ and have trusted him as your Savior, your salvation has been made secure by the Spirit of God (Eph. 1:13; 4:30). But the devil is like a little weasel. He'll do whatever he can to prevent you from enjoying heaven to the fullest extent. Don't let him.

The Devil's Device

So what tricks does Satan have in his bag? Plenty, but he rarely needs them all. For most of us, one trick is enough. Not temptation, greed, or jealousy. Those are too obvious. To rob you of eternal reward the devil uses something far more subtle—diversion.

Satan didn't stop attacking you when you became a member of the family of God. He just shifted his emphasis. He doesn't try to lead believers astray as much as he tries to lead them aside, getting them wrapped up in trivial pursuits. When he succeeds, he keeps us from valuable service and from greater eternal reward.

Richard Baxter, the great Puritan preacher of the seventeenth century, asked, "What have we our time and strength for, but to lay both out for God?" He's right. We've been saved to serve our Lord. We are the workmanship of God, "created in Christ Jesus for good works, which God prepared beforehand, that we should walk in them" (Eph. 2:10).

The devil doesn't always try to keep us from the good works God has prepared for us. He doesn't have to. Instead he drags red herrings across our path, gets us off into spiritual cul-de-sacs. He lets other things become more important to us. He gets us bogged down in what seems like good activity, but is really meaningless with respect to eternity. He's very clever that way.

Diverted Demas

A good example of someone the devil diverted is Demas. We know very little about him; Demas is mentioned only three times in Scripture. In his letter to Philemon, Paul indicates that he is anxious to say hello to those who have labored with him for the gospel. He concludes this short letter by saying, "Epaphras, my fellow prisoner in Christ Jesus, sends greetings to you, and so do Mark, Aristarchus, Demas, and Luke, my fellow workers" (Philem. 23–24). This gives us evidence that Demas was a worker with Paul and was engaged in spreading the gospel wherever he went. Again, in the closing verse of Colossians, Demas is mentioned in the select company of Aristarchus, Mark, Justus, Epaphras, and Luke (Col. 4:14). That's pretty good company!

The third and final reference to Demas is found in the last letter the apostle ever wrote—2 Timothy. From his writing you can tell that Paul is aging, sickly, and nearing death. It's in this state that Paul writes, "For Demas, in love with this present world, has deserted me and gone to Thessalonica" (4:10). There it is. A fifteen-word description of Demas that will endure for eternity (Ps. 119:89).

It's not likely that Demas abandoned the faith. Paul doesn't indicate that his friend fell into some sort of sin. Paul simply said Demas had forsaken him because he was "in love with this present world." Perhaps Demas returned to Thessalonica to become a junior partner in his father's business. Maybe he had a job offer that would pay well and still permit him to be an outstanding Christian citizen of Greece. There is no hint that Demas did anything illegal, immoral, or wrong. He was just diverted to something of lesser eternal importance.

What happened to Demas happens to far too many Christians. Maybe it's happened to you—you've had the unfortunate experience of becoming content with just being a Christian. You go to church and get your weekly spiritual buzz, but you're not changed, motivated to serve, energized to make an eternal difference. You've become sidetracked, bogged down, diverted, empty.

Remember, Satan doesn't have to defeat you—he only has to divert you. Is his plan working? Look around you. Do you have a ton of stuff but little to show for your life? Are you busy at the gym, the club, even at church, but you have nothing of eternal value to show for it? What about your checkbook or debit card? How do they reflect your priorities? Do you see any evidence of beginning your day at the judgment seat of Christ and working backward? Is the devil diverting you, sidetracking you from living with eternity in view?

Good Advice

Jesus gives us some very poignant advice when he says, "Do not lay up for yourselves treasures on earth, where moth and rust destroy and where thieves break in and steal, but lay up for yourselves treasures in heaven, where neither moth nor rust destroys and where thieves do not break in and steal. For where your treasure is, there your heart will be also" (Matt. 6:19–21). I don't know any better advice than that.

The Lord Jesus is speaking about your priorities; what's most important in your life? If you spend all of your time gathering treasures (rewards) on earth, how do you expect to have any time left to gather treasures (rewards) for heaven? Is it more important that you live the good life, or that lives are changed for good? Is it more important that you invest your money in Wall Street or in the eternal work of the Lord? What really is most important to you? And where does the priority of the judgment seat of Christ fit in your list of today's priorities?

Starting every day at the judgment seat of Christ and working backwards means your start there and work back to your Blackberry, your calendar, your checkbook, your "to do" list. How does what you do today change what you will enjoy for all eternity? Start at the judgment seat—every day.

One day we'll all face our final job review. We'll give account to our Master of our lives. Are you ready? When you face your final job review, all chance to earn rewards will be behind you. So today is your day. It presents the chance of a lifetime. Who knows, it may be your last chance of a lifetime. Don't squander it.

What have you learned in this book that could help you face that final review with anticipation and confidence? Remember, "Whatever your hand finds to do, do it with your might, for there is no work or thought or knowledge or wisdom in Sheol, to which you are going" (Eccles. 9:10). Whatever you do today that has no impact on eternity is a waste of today. Start at the judgment seat. Work backwards. Live confidently.

NOTES

Chapter 2: How Are Rewards Different from Salvation?

1. Dante Alighieri, *The Divine Comedy: Inferno; Purgatorio; Paradiso* (New York: Knopf [Everyman's Library], 1995).

Chapter 3: Should I Be Concerned about Eternal Rewards?

1. The seven deadly sins are lust, gluttony, greed, sloth, wrath, envy, and pride.

2. Alan Greenspan, quoted in Caroline Overington, "'Infectious Greed' the New Corporate Sin: Greenspan," Happiness Online, July 8, 2002. http://www.happinessonline.org/InfectiousGreed/p2.htm.

Chapter 5: Who Are Judged at the Judgment Seat?

1. "For we know that if the tent that is our earthly home is destroyed, we have a building from God, a house not made with hands, eternal in the heavens. For in this tent we groan, longing to put on our heavenly dwelling, if indeed by putting it on we may not be found naked. For while we are still in this tent, we groan, being burdened—not that we would be unclothed, but that we would be further clothed, so that what is mortal may be swallowed up by life. He who has prepared us for this very thing is God, who has given us the Spirit as a guarantee. So we are always of good courage. We know that while we are at home in the body we are away from the Lord, for we walk by faith, not by sight. Yes, we are of good courage, and we would rather be away from the body and at home with the Lord. So whether we are at home or away, we make it our aim to please him. For we must all appear before the judgment seat of Christ, so that each one may receive what is due for what he has done in the body, whether good or evil" (2 Cor. 5:1–10).

Chapter 6: Who Is the Judge?

1. Jesus taught, "The Father judges no one, but has given all judgment to the Son, that all may honor the Son, just as they honor the Father. Whoever does not honor the Son does not honor the Father who sent him" (John 5:22–23).

Chapter 7: When Will the Judgment Take Place?

1. The tribulation period is that future time between the Lord's return for his church and his second coming to earth in power and glory at the Battle of Armageddon. It will be a time of unprecedented trouble for the world (Jer. 30:7; Matt. 24:21–22, 29). Those who have not followed Christ will suffer from intense divine judgments, Israel will be persecuted severely, and Gentiles who do follow Christ will be martyred. The entire period will be seven years long and will be that part of the Day of the Lord when God will judge his enemies and establish a new world order (see Isa. 13:6–16; Joel 2:1–11, 28–32; Zeph. 1:7–2:3; Zech. 14:1–13; 1 Thess. 5:1–9; 2 Thess. 2:1–3 [in Greek]; and 2 Peter 3:10).

Chapter 8: Where Will the Judgment Seat Be?

1. When John received the Revelation it wasn't just about things that would take place in the future here on earth. It also was about a new future with a new heaven and a new earth. He wrote, "Then I saw a new heaven and a new earth, for the first heaven and the first earth had passed away, and the sea was no more (Rev. 21:1). The apostle Peter informs us that this new heaven and new earth will appear after the present heaven and earth are purged from sin (2 Peter 3:10–13). Following the judgment on this earth called the Day of the Lord (Isa. 13:10–13; Joel 2:1–2, 30–31), God will create a restored heaven and earth, a glorious place for the righteous to dwell. Read about it in Revelation 21 and 22.

Chapter 9: Why Would God Judge Me?

1. There are many judgments mentioned throughout the Bible. Some of them are still future, but don't relate to those who have come to faith in Christ as Savior. Major judgments of the future that do not relate to the follower of Christ are: (1) the judgment of Israel—a judgment of the Jews during the tribulation to come (Ezek. 39:29; Zechariah 14); (2) the judgment of the nations—when Jesus purges the earth of rebels at the close of the tribulation period (Matthew 25); and (3) the great white throne judgment—commonly called "the great judgment day" that results in the eternal damnation of those who have rejected the Lord Jesus Christ (Revelation 20).

Chapter 10: Does Judgment Mean I'll Be Condemned?

1. H. A. Ironside, *Addresses on the Second Epistle to the Corinthians* (Neptune, NJ: Loizeaux Brothers, 1964), 134–35.

Notes

Chapter 11: What Is the Purpose of Heaven's Judgment Seat?

1. John Piper, "What Happens When You Die? 'All Appear Before the Judgment Seat of Christ,' 2 Corinthians 5:1–10," Sound of Grace, Aug. 1, 1993. http://soundofgrace.com/piper93/8-1-93.htm.

2. A mina was a Greek coin equal to one hundred denarii in Roman coins. A denarius was the equivalent of a common laborer's wage for one day's work. The mina, therefore, was equal to about three month's salary and was a considerable amount of money.

Chapter 15: Is There Real Fire at the Evaluation?

1. Erwin Lutzer, *Your Eternal Reward* (Chicago: Moody, 1998), 65.

Chapter 16: Is It Possible to Lose Rewards?

1. E. Schuyler English, "The Church at the Tribunal," in *Prophetic Truth Unfolding Today*, ed. Charles Lee Feinberg (Old Tappan, NJ: Revell, 1968), 29.

Chapter 18: What If I Haven't Chosen Gold?

1. Exodus 28:15–21, "You shall make a breastpiece of judgment, in skilled work. In the style of the ephod you shall make it—of gold, blue and purple and scarlet yarns, and fine twined linen shall you make it. It shall be square and doubled, a span its length and a span its breadth. You shall set in it four rows of stones. A row of sardius, topaz, and carbuncle shall be the first row; and the second row an emerald, a sapphire, and a diamond; and the third row a jacinth, an agate, and an amethyst; and the fourth row a beryl, an onyx, and a jasper. They shall be set in gold filigree. There shall be twelve stones with their names according to the names of the sons of Israel. They shall be like signets, each engraved with its name, for the twelve tribes."

Chapter 20: Does My Faithfulness Count?

1. "Employee Absenteeism," Profiles International. http://www.profilesinternational.com/SYC_absenteeism.aspx.

2. Information on the total numbers and rates of marriages and divorces at the national and state levels are published in the National Center for Health Statistics' National Vital Statistics Report. However, these numbers do not include states that no longer record such data, such as California, Georgia, Hawaii, Indiana, Louisiana, and Minnesota.

3. J. Budziszewski, "Virtual Unfaithfulness: Pornography Use in a Marriage," Pure Intimacy. http://www.pureintimacy.org/cs/couples/a0000083.cfm.

Chapter 21: What If I Have Limited Opportunity or Ability?

1. Erwin Lutzer, *Your Eternal Reward* (Chicago: Moody, 1998), 37–38.

2. Adapted from his life story in Rackham Holt, *George Washington Carver: An American Biography* (New York: Doubleday, 1963).

Chapter 25: What about Reigning with Christ?

1. There are those who understand the "overcomer" to be in a special category of super saints, those who have engaged in a deeper life with God that the ordinary Christ-follower knows nothing about. They say that overcomers alone are permitted to enter the kingdom of God, while other believers are kept out because of their inferior relationship with God. But this is not the case. In his kingdom, Christ doesn't have a Christian caste system like the Hindu caste system in which some are "outcasts." "Overcomer" is a general description of what a normative life of service to the Lord should be like. It is a description of all who are true followers of Jesus Christ. The apostle John asked and answered a pertinent question in his first epistle: "Who is it that overcomes the world except the one who believes that Jesus is the Son of God?" (1 John 5:5). While the judgment seat will determine our place of service in Christ's millennial kingdom, it will never exclude those who belong there from being there.

Chapter 26: What's All This about Crowns in Heaven?

1. The apocryphal book of Maccabees (1:14) informs us that the Seleucid king, Antiochus Epiphanes, built a gymnasium in Jerusalem. Later Herod the Great erected a theater and amphitheater both at Jerusalem and Caesarea where races, gymnastics, etc., were held. The amphitheater at Caesarea is wonderfully preserved, though not excavated, and can be seen today.

2. The Pan-Hellenic Games was a series of four games held during the Olympiad, the four-year period associated with the Olympic Games. The four games were the Olympics, held every four years near Elis in honor of Zeus; the Pythian Games, held every four years near Delphi in honor of Apollo; the Nemean Games, held every two years near Nemea in honor of Zeus; and the Isthmian Games, held every two years near Corinth in honor of Poseidon.

3. Every four years most of us are glued to our televisions watching the Olympic Games. That event is a reminder that the Olympics apparently began in 776 BC at ancient Olympia. Although the Romans orchestrated the games in Paul's day, they had about the same flavor as given them by the ancient Greeks. Most of Paul's knowledge of ancient athletic contests came directly from his travels in Greece. The Olympic Games, as well as the other Pan-Hellenic games, flourished until the time of Theodosius 1 in AD 393 or his grandson Theodosius II in AD 435, when all such games were suppressed as being pagan.

4. In his *Isthmian Odes* (bk 2, line 16 and bk 8, line 64), the greatest of the lyric poets of ancient Greece, Pindar, indicated that the winners of the Isthmian games received a wreath of celery adorning their head instead of olive or laurel. At first the

Romans shunned the idea of wearing wreaths. However, they retained a fascination with the idea, and soon the upper classes were wearing garlands of oak, laurel, and olive leaves. When Julius Caesar was crowned, it was with a wreath of fresh laurel. Eventually wreaths gave way to crowns, which were created for royalty. The word "crown" is derived from the Latin word *corona*, which means garland or wreath.

SCRIPTURE INDEX